Dinner *and a* Movie

Printed in the United States of America
by G&R Publishing Co.

Distributed By:

507 Industrial Street
Waverly, IA 50677

ISBN-13: 978-1-56383-232-1
ISBN-10: 1-56383-232-1
Item #7021

Table of Contents

Introduction

Welcome to Dinner and a Movie — the cookbook that combines the thrilling, romantic, adventurous and dramatic stories of Oscar-winning movies with a main dish recipe that is a perfect companion to the movie theme. Use this book to create great memories for family nights, date nights, sleepovers, movie parties or just hanging out with friends. Everyone will enjoy the idea of preparing and serving a meal that relates to the film being shown.

In this book, the left hand side of each page highlights an Oscar award-winning movie and lists the movie type, rating, length, cast members, reason for winning an Oscar and a short movie description. On the facing page, you will find the ingredients and directions for a recipe that complements the movie listed. While it may be obvious why some recipes were chosen to accompany the movie, others may leave you baffled — until you watch the feature film, that is. Part of the fun can be in figuring out why each recipe ties in with the movie.

Encourage your friends and family to get creative by cooking up side dishes or desserts that accompany each movie. For example, who could watch Forrest Gump without serving some Dr. Pepper and a box of chocolates? Or how about chewing on some tasty Tootsie Rolls while viewing Tootsie? You get the idea... you are only one movie rental away from having a delicious and fun Dinner and a Movie night!

The Academy

If you've ever watched the Academy Awards (informally known as the Oscars), then you've probably heard people giving "Thanks to the Academy." But what does that mean?

The Academy of Motion Picture Arts and Sciences (AMPAS) is a professional honorary organization dedicated to the advancement of the arts and sciences of motion pictures. AMPAS was founded on May 11, 1927 in California by 36 members, and now has more than 6,000 motion picture professionals as members. While the majority of AMPAS members are from the United States, membership is open to qualified filmmakers around the world. As of 2004, the Academy included theatrical filmmakers from 36 countries on its roster.

The Academy is most widely recognized for its annual Academy Awards – an elaborate ceremony where awards are given to recognize films and persons the Academy believes have the top achievement in motion picture arts and sciences of the year. In addition, the Academy gives annual Student Academy Awards to filmmakers at the undergraduate and graduate level, awards up to five annual Nicholl Fellowships in Screenwriting, and operates the Margaret Herrick Library in Beverly Hills, California and the Pickford Center for Motion Picture Study in Hollywood, California.

The Academy Awards

The Academy Awards are the most prominent film awards in the United States, and the most-watched awards ceremony in the world. Most would agree that an Academy Award is the most prestigious award anyone in the film business can win.

The first Academy Awards were handed out on May 16, 1929 at a banquet ceremony held in the Blossom Room of the Hollywood Roosevelt Hotel. The attendance was 270 and tickets cost $5.

The first 15 Awards presentations were banquet affairs held in hotel banquet rooms. After 1942, increased attendance and World War II made banquets impractical and the Awards moved to theaters, where they've been held since.

The Academy Awards were first televised on March 19, 1953. The NBC-TV and radio network carried the 25th Academy Awards ceremonies live from Hollywood with Bob Hope emceeing.

The winners at each ceremony are presented with a golden statuette, known as an Oscar. One popular, but unsubstantiated, story notes that the award was named by an Academy librarian and eventual executive director, Margaret Herrick, who said the statuette resembled her Uncle Oscar. Its first documented mention came after the sixth Awards Presentation in 1934, when Hollywood columnist Sidney Skolsky used it in reference to Katharine Hepburn's first Best Actress win. The Academy itself didn't use the nickname officially until 1939.

Oscar Facts

In the first year of the Academy Awards, there were two "Outstanding Picture" winners: Wings (1927/28) for Best Production, and Sunrise (1927) for Unique and Artistic Picture. The second category was later dropped from the awards ceremony.

Three awards were given during the Academy's first year that were never given again, including: Best Artistic Quality of Production, Best Title Writing (for silent films), and Best Comedy Direction. The only silent film to ever win Best Picture was Wings.

Two Best Picture winning films, Titanic (1997) and All About Eve (1950) both hold the record for the most nominations earned by a single film, with 14. Five Best Picture films are tied for second place with 13 nominations, including Gone With the Wind (1939), From Here to Eternity (1953), Shakespeare in Love (1998), Forrest Gump (1994) and Chicago (2002).

The three Best Picture winning films with the most Oscar wins include: The Lord of the Rings: The Return of the King (2003), Titanic (1997), and Ben-Hur (1959). Each of these films won 11 Oscars. West Side Story won 10 Oscars out of a total 11 nominations.

All Quiet on the Western Front

Movie Type: Drama/War
Year: 1930

Rating: Not Rated   Length: 130 minutes

Cast includes:

Lewis Ayres, Louis Wolheim, George Summerville, Beryl Mercer and more

And the Oscar goes to...

☆ **Best Picture**
☆ **Best Director, Lewis Milestone**

Brief movie overview

Based on Erich Maria Remarques' anti-war novel, this ground breaking film presented war in a whole new light. The movie tells the story of Paul, an eager young German man who enthusiastically enlists in Kaiser's army in World War I. In scene after scene, the stark and ugly reality of trench warfare unfolds. This movie truly defines the anti-war genre and has influenced generations of war films.

Wiener Schnitzel

2 lbs. veal
1 C. flour
4 eggs
1 T. vegetable oil

Salt and pepper to taste
4 C. bread crumbs
2 T. oil for frying

Cut veal into ½″ to ¾″ thick steaks. Dredge in flour. In a shallow dish, beat eggs with vegetable oil, salt and pepper. In another shallow dish, place bread crumbs. Coat the steaks with egg mixture and then coat with bread crumbs. Place 2 tablespoons oil in a heavy skillet over medium heat. Fry veal until golden brown, approximately 5 minutes on each side.

Gone with the Wind

Movie Type: Romance/Epic
Year: 1939

Rating: G

Length: 222 minutes

Cast includes:

Vivien Leigh, Clark Gable, Leslie Howard, Olivia de Havilland, Hattie McDaniel and more

And the Oscar goes to...

☆ Best Picture
☆ Best Actress, Vivien Leigh
☆ Best Supporting Actress, Hattie McDaniel
☆ Best Director, Victor Fleming
☆ Also won for Art Direction, Cinematography, Film Editing, Screenplay, among others

Brief movie overview

A spoiled Southern girl falls hopelessly in love with a married man. Scarlett O'Hara tries to lure her beau, Ashley Wilkes, from the "mealy mouthed" Melanie Hamilton. When she throws herself at Wilkes, her fit of histrionics is witnessed by Rhett Butler, the black sheep of a wealthy Charleston family. Butler is instantly fascinated by the feisty, self-centered O'Hara. "We're bad lots, both of us."

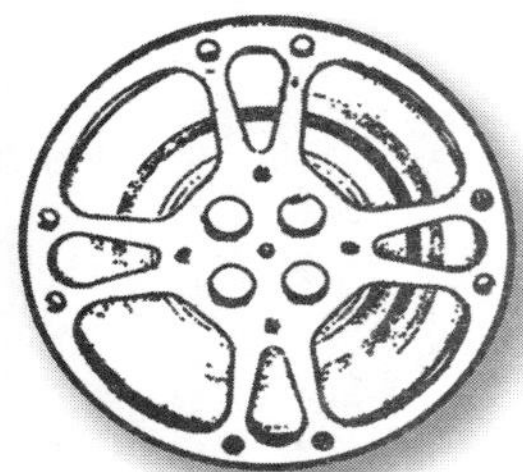

Chicken Fried Steak

Accompany the movie with this true-blue Southern dish.

¼ tsp. salt
¼ tsp. pepper
4 (4 oz.) cube steaks
38 saltine crackers, crushed
1¼ C. flour, divided
½ tsp. baking powder

2 tsp. salt, divided
1½ tsp. pepper, divided
½ tsp. cayenne pepper
4¾ C. milk, divided
2 eggs
3½ C. peanut oil

Preheat oven to 225°. Sprinkle salt and pepper evenly over steaks. Set aside. In a shallow bowl, combine cracker crumbs, 1 cup flour, baking powder, 1 teaspoon salt, ½ teaspoon pepper and cayenne pepper. In another shallow bowl, whisk together ¾ cup milk and eggs. Dredge steaks in cracker crumb mixture then dip in egg mixture. Dredge steaks in cracker crumb mixture again. Pour oil onto a 12″ skillet and heat to medium-high heat (non-stick skillets are not advised). Fry steaks for 10 minutes on the first side then turn and fry for 4 to 5 additional minutes or until golden brown. Remove steaks and place in oven to keep warm. Carefully drain hot oil from skillet, reserving cooked bits and 1 tablespoon drippings. In a bowl, whisk together remaining ¼ cup flour, 1 teaspoon salt, 1 teaspoon pepper and 4 cups milk. Pour mixture into skillet with reserved drippings. Whisk constantly over medium-high heat for 10 to 12 minutes or until mixture is thickened. Serve gravy with steaks. Mashed potatoes make an excellent side with this dish.

Casablanca

Movie Type: Drama/Romance
Year: 1942

Rating: PG   Length: 102 minutes

Cast includes:

Humphrey Bogart, Ingrid Bergman, Paul Henreid, Claude Rains, Conrad Veidt and more

And the Oscar goes to...

✷ **Best Picture**
✷ **Best Director, Michael Curtiz**
✷ **Best Screenplay, Julius Epstein, Philip Epstein and Howard Koch**

Brief movie overview

An American expatriate meets a former lover, with unforeseen complications. This classic film is set in occupied Africa during the early days of World War II.

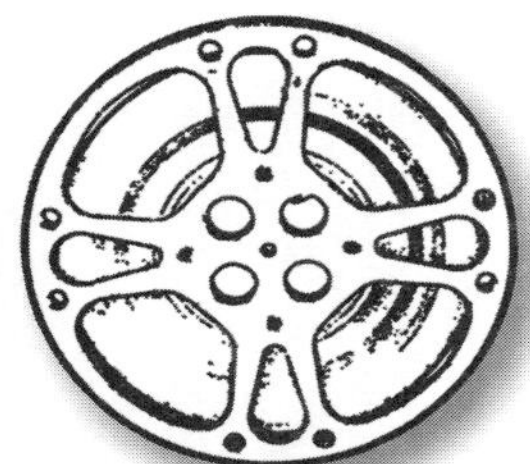

Play it Again Salmon

2 cloves garlic, minced
6 T. light olive oil
1 tsp. dried basil
1 tsp. salt

1 tsp. pepper
1 T. lemon juice
1 T. fresh parsley, chopped
2 (6 oz.) salmon fillets

In a medium bowl, prepare marinade by mixing garlic, olive oil, basil, salt, pepper, lemon juice and parsley. Place salmon fillets in a medium glass baking dish and cover with marinade. Marinate fillets in the refrigerator for 1 hour, turning occasionally. Preheat oven to 375°. Place fillets on squares of aluminum foil, cover with marinade and bring up sides, folding to seal packets. Place the sealed foil packets in a glass dish and bake for 35 to 45 minutes until salmon is easily flaked with a fork.

Miracle on 34th Street

Movie Type: Comedy/Drama/Fantasy/Romance
Year: 1947

Rating: Approved   Length: 96 minutes

Cast includes:

Maureen O'Hara, John Payne, Edmund Gwenn, Gene Lockhart and more

And the Oscar goes to...

☆ **Best Supporting Actor, Edmund Gwenn**
☆ **Best Motion Picture Story, Valentine Davies**
☆ **Best Screenplay, George Seaton**

Brief movie overview

A nice old man is institutionalized as insane after his claim to be Santa Claus. A young lawyer decides to defend him by arguing in court that he is the real thing.

Maple and Mustard Glazed Roast Pork

Serve this classic holiday dish to get everyone in a festive spirit.

1 C. real maple syrup
4 T. Dijon mustard
2½ T. cider vinegar

2½ T. soy sauce
Salt and pepper to taste
2½ lbs. boneless pork loin

Preheat oven to 350°. In a small bowl, mix maple syrup, mustard, vinegar, soy sauce and salt and pepper. Set aside. Place pork loin in a shallow roasting pan. Spread glaze evenly over pork. Cook until loin has an internal temperature of 160°, approximately 45 minutes to 1½ hours. Remove from oven and let cool for 10 minutes before serving.

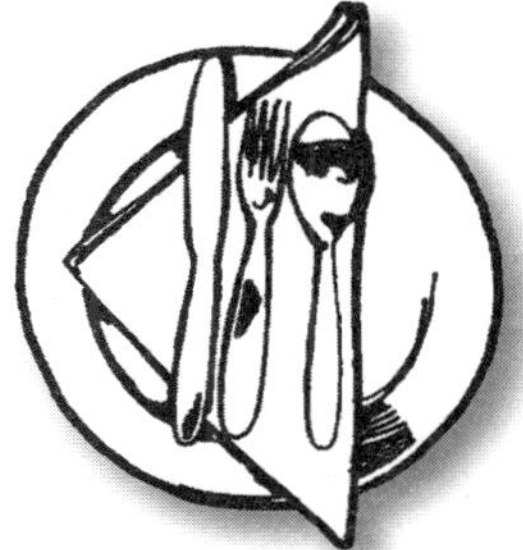

High Noon

Movie Type: Thriller/Western
Year: 1952

Rating: Approved   Length: 85 minutes

Cast includes:

Gary Cooper, Thomas Mitchell, Lloyd Bridges, Katy Jurado, Grace Kelly and more

And the Oscar goes to...

★ **Best Actor, Gary Cooper**
★ **Film Editing, Elmo Williams and Harry Gerstad**
★ **Best Music Score, Dimitri Tiomkin**
★ **Best Song, "High Noon", music by Dimitri Tiomkin,**
   lyrics by Ned Washington

Brief movie overview

Will Kane, serving his last day as marshal, is about to leave town with his new bride. Though, an outlaw who was formerly imprisoned by Kane plans to return to town with his gang. Kane doesn't want to flee from the outlaws and tries to find support from his friends, but they are too afraid and leave Kane all alone to defend the town.

BBQ Ribs

Enjoy this western "mesquite" BBQ flavor during the flick!

2½ lbs. country style pork ribs
1 T. garlic powder
1 tsp. pepper

2 T. salt
1 C. barbeque sauce, any kind

In a large pot, place ribs. Cover ribs with water and season with garlic powder, pepper and salt. Bring water to a boil and cook ribs until tender, approximately 1 hour. Preheat oven to 325°. Remove ribs from pot and place in a 9 x 13″ baking dish. Pour barbeque sauce over ribs. Cover dish with aluminum foil and bake for 1 to 1½ hours or until ribs have an internal temperature of 160°.

The Greatest Show on Earth

Movie Type: Drama/Family/Romance
Year: 1952

Rating: Not Rated   Length: 152 minutes

Cast includes:

Betty Hutton, Cornel Wilde, Charlton Heston, Dorothy Lamour, Gloria Grahame and more

And the Oscar goes to...

☆ **Best Picture**
☆ **Best Writing, Frederic Frank, Theodore John and Frank Cavett**

Brief movie overview

The details of the dramatic lives of trapeze artists, a clown and an elephant trainer against a background of circus spectacle. The circus manager's girlfriend, Holly, and The Great Sebastian, begin a dangerous one-upmanship duel in the show ring.

Homemade Corn Dogs

1 qt. oil for deep frying
1 C. flour
⅔ C. cornmeal
¼ C. sugar
1½ tsp. baking powder
1 tsp. salt
2 T. bacon drippings, melted

1 egg, beaten
1¼ C. buttermilk
½ tsp. baking soda
2 lbs. hot dogs
Wooden dowels
 or skewers

Heat oil in a deep fryer to 365°. In a large bowl, mix together flour, cornmeal, sugar, baking powder and salt. Stir in bacon drippings. Form a well in the center and add egg, buttermilk and baking soda. Mix until batter is smooth and well-blended. To ensure hot dogs are completely dry, pat with paper towels. Insert wooden skewers into one end of each hot dog. Dip hot dogs in batter one at a time, shaking off excess. Deep fry 2 to 3 corn dogs at one time until they are golden brown. Drain on paper towels and serve.

On the Waterfront

Movie Type: Drama/Romance
Year: 1954

Rating: Approved   Length: 108 minutes

Cast includes:

Marlon Brando, Karl Malden, Lee Cobb, Rod Steiger and more

And the Oscar goes to...

☆ **Best Picture**
☆ **Best Actor, Marlon Brando**
☆ **Best Supporting Actress, Eva Marie Saint**
☆ **Art Direction, Richard Day**
☆ **Best Director, Elia Kazan**
☆ **Also won for Cinematography, Film Editing and Screenplay**

Brief movie overview

Terry Malloy, an ex-prize fighter turned longshoreman, struggles to stand up to his corrupt union bosses. Malloy witnesses a murder and later meets the dead man's sister. She introduces him to Father Barry, who tries to force him to provide information that will bring the dock swindlers down.

Fish with a Punch

2 C. dry potato flakes
1 C. flour
1 T. garlic powder
1 T. seasoning salt
1 T. pepper

2 tsp. cayenne pepper, or to taste
4 (6 oz.) cod fillets
2 C. butter flavored shortening for frying

In a shallow bowl, combine the potato flakes, flour, garlic powder, seasoning salt, pepper and cayenne pepper. Soak fillets in a bowl of cold water. In a deep skillet or a deep fryer, melt and heat shortening to 350°. Dredge fillets in dry mixture and fry, turning once, for 5 minutes or until fish flakes easily. Remove from oil and place on paper towels to drain.

The King & I

Movie Type: Adventure/Drama/Musical/Romance
Year: 1956

Rating: G   Length: 133 minutes

Cast includes:

Deborah Kerr, Yul Brynner, Rita Moreno, Martin Benson, Terry Saunders and more

And the Oscar goes to...

☆ Best Actor, Yul Brynner
☆ Art Direction, Lyle Wheeler, John DeCuir, Walter Scott and Paul Fox
☆ Also won for Costume Design, Music and Sound Recording

Brief movie overview

A musical about a widow who accepts a job as a live-in governess for the children of the King of Siam in Bangkok. The governess, Mrs. Anna Leonowens, has been contracted to teach English to the children of the royal household. A tangled tale of love develops.

Crispy Thai Spring Rolls

2 T. regular soy sauce

2 T. fish sauce

2 T. lime juice

¼ tsp. sugar

2 T. oil for stir-frying

3 cloves garlic, minced

2 oz. ginger, grated

2 shallots, thinly sliced

1 red chili, seeded and finely sliced

½ C. shredded cabbage

4 to 6 shiitake mushrooms, sliced thinly

½ C. tofu, cut into matchstick-size pieces

2 C. bean sprouts

½ C. fresh coriander, coarsely chopped

½ C. fresh basil, coarsely chopped

1 pkg. small spring roll wrappers

Additional oil for frying

In a medium bowl, mix first 4 ingredients. Set aside. In a wok or large skillet, heat oil over medium-high heat. Add garlic, ginger, shallots and chili. Stir-fry for 1 minute. If needed, add a bit of water to the wok to avoid dryness. Add cabbage, mushrooms and tofu. Stir-fry for 1 to 2 minutes or until vegetables have softened. Add bean sprouts and toss to mix. Remove from heat. To assemble rolls, place one heaping tablespoon of the filling into each of the spring roll wrappers and spread lengthwise along the wrapper. Sprinkle fresh coriander and basil over each. For each spring roll, fold the short ends over the filling then lift up the end closest to you, fold over top and roll to the other end. Secure by pasting it shut with a bit of water. Place additional oil approximately 1˝ deep in a wok over medium-high heat. Using tongs, place spring rolls in oil that is slightly bubbling. Allow rolls to fry for 1 minute on each side or until golden brown. Place on paper towels to drain. Mix the dipping sauce ingredients until well combined. Serve rolls with sauce.

Dipping Sauce:

⅓ C. plum sauce

2 T. soy sauce

1 T. fish sauce

Gigi

Movie Type: Comedy/Musical/Romance
Year: 1958

Rating: PG   Length: 119 minutes

Cast includes:

Leslie Caron, Maurice Chevalier, Louis Jourdan, Hermione Gingold, Eva Gabor and more

And the Oscar goes to...

* Best Picture
* Best Director, Vincente Minnelli
* Art Direction, William Horning, Preston Ames, Henry Grace and Keogh Gleason
* Also won for Cinematography, Costume Design, Film Editing, Music and Screenplay

Brief movie overview

In turn-of-the-century Paris, Gaston Lachaille, a rich bon vivant, and Gigi, a youthful courtesan-in-training, enjoy a platonic friendship. But it doesn't stay platonic for long...

Chicken Cordon Bleu

4 skinless, boneless chicken
  breast halves
¼ tsp. salt
⅛ tsp. pepper

6 slices Swiss cheese
4 slices cooked ham
½ C. seasoned bread crumbs

Preheat oven to 350°. Pound chicken breasts to ¼″ thickness. Sprinkle each breast with salt and pepper. Place 1 cheese slice and 1 ham slice on top of each piece of chicken. Roll up and secure each breast with a toothpick. Place in a greased baking dish and sprinkle chicken evenly with bread crumbs. Bake for 30 to 35 minutes or until chicken is no longer pink. Remove from oven and place a half a slice of cheese on top of each roll. Return to oven for 3 to 5 minutes or until cheese is melted. Remove toothpicks and serve.

The Alamo

Movie Type: Adventure/Drama/Western
Year: 1960

Rating: PG   Length: 167 minutes

Cast includes:

John Wayne, Richard Widmark, Laurence Harvey, Frankie Avalon and more

And the Oscar goes to...

☆ Best Sound, Samuel Goldwyn Studio Sound

Brief movie overview

The legendary true story of a small band of soldiers who sacrificed their lives in hopeless combat against a massive army. Their ambition is to prevent a tyrant from smashing the new Republic of Texas.

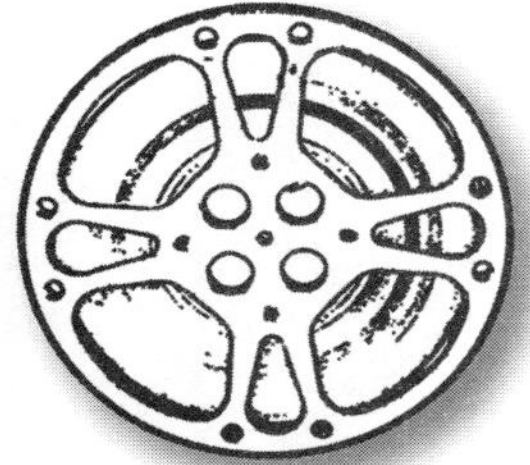

Chicken Enchiladas

1 T. butter
½ C. chopped green onions
½ tsp. garlic powder
1 (4 oz.) can diced
  green chilies
1 (10¾ oz.) can cream
  of mushroom soup

½ C. sour cream
1½ C. cubed cooked
  chicken breast
1 C. shredded Cheddar
  cheese, divided
6 (12˝) flour tortillas
¼ C. milk

Preheat oven to 350°. In a medium saucepan over medium heat, melt butter. Add onions and sauté until tender. Add garlic powder, chilies, mushroom soup and sour cream. Mix until well combined. Reserve ¾ of the sauce and set aside. Add chicken and half of the shredded cheese to the remaining sauce and mix well. Fill each tortilla with chicken mixture and roll up. Place filled tortillas, seam side down, in a lightly greased baking dish. In a small bowl, combine reserved sauce with milk until well mixed. Spoon over filled tortillas and top with the remaining cheese. Bake for 30 to 35 minutes, or until cheese is bubbly.

Never on Sunday

Movie Type: Comedy/Drama
Year: 1960

Rating: PG   Length: 97 minutes

Cast includes:

Melina Mercouri, Jules Dassin, George Foundas, Titos Vandis and more

And the Oscar goes to...

☆ Best Song, "Never on Sunday", music and lyrics
  by Manos Hadjidakis

Brief movie overview

An American scholar in Greece believes the country has fallen from ancient greatness. He decides that Illia, a popular energetic prostitute, is a symbol of that fall and he sets out to study, improve and save her.

Italian Calzones

1 (¼ oz.) pkg. active
   dry yeast
1 T. plus 1 tsp. olive oil,
   divided
1 tsp. sugar
1 tsp. salt
2½ C. flour, divided

½ C. ricotta cheese
1½ C. shredded
   Cheddar cheese
½ C. diced pepperoni
½ C. sliced fresh mushrooms
1 T. dried basil leaves
1 egg, beaten

In a small bowl, dissolve yeast in 1 cup warm water. Add 1 tablespoon oil, sugar and salt. Mix in 1 cup flour until smooth. Gradually stir in the remaining flour until dough is workable and smooth. On a lightly floured surface, knead dough for 5 minutes or until it is elastic. In a medium bowl, place 1 teaspoon olive oil. Place dough in olive oil then turn to coat. Cover and let rise for 40 minutes or until almost doubled in size. While dough is rising, in a large bowl, combine the cheeses, pepperoni, mushrooms and basil leaves. Mix well, cover and refrigerate. Preheat oven to 375°. When dough is ready, punch it down and separate into two equal pieces. Roll each piece into thin circles on a lightly floured surface. Fill each circle with half of the filling and fold over, securing edges by folding in and pressing with a fork. Brush the top of each calzone with egg and place on a lightly greased baking sheet. Bake for 30 minutes.

Breakfast at Tiffany's

Movie Type: Drama/Romance
Year: 1961

Rating: Not Rated   Length: 115 minutes

Cast includes:

Audrey Hepburn, George Peppard, Patricia Neal, Buddy Ebsen and more

And the Oscar goes to...

☆ Best Music Score, Henry Mancini
☆ Best Song, "Moon River", music by Henry Mancini, lyrics by Johnny Mercer

Brief movie overview

Based on Truman Capote's novella, this is a story of a young New York socialite who becomes interested in a young writer who has moved into her apartment building.

Eggs Benedict

1⅓ C. butter
2 large egg yolks
1 T. strained freshly-
  squeezed lemon juice
1 tsp. kosher salt
Pinch of white pepper or
  cayenne pepper

½ C. distilled vinegar,
  divided
12 large eggs
1 T. unsalted butter
12 slices
  Canadian bacon
6 plain English muffins, split

To prepare, in a small pan, melt butter. Remove from heat and set aside for 5 minutes. Skim and discard any white foam that forms on the surface of the butter. Set aside. Fill a medium saucepan with 2˝ water and bring to a simmer. In a medium heat-proof bowl, combine egg yolks and 2 tablespoons cold water. Whisk until yolks are light and frothy. Place bowl over simmering water and whisk vigorously until yolks are thickened and light, about 3 to 4 minutes (remove from heat if eggs start to scramble). Remove bowl from heat and whisk for 30 seconds to cool. Remove water from heat and once again set the bowl over hot water. Slowly drizzle butter into eggs, constantly whisking. Whisk in lemon juice, salt and pepper. Sauce should be creamy and light (add a few drops of water if needed) and can be kept warm by placing over a bowl of warm water. Fill 2 large skillets with water to reach a depth of 3˝ then divide the vinegar between them. Bring both skillets to a simmer. Crack each egg into a cup then slide it into the hot liquid. Poach eggs, turning occasionally with a spoon, for 3 to 5 minutes or until the whites are firm. Remove eggs and transfer to a towel to soak up excess water. While eggs are poaching, melt butter in a large skillet, add Canadian bacon and cook for 1 minute on each side. To serve, toast the muffins and top each half with a slice of Canadian bacon and poached egg. Spoon sauce over all.

Cleopatra

Movie Type: Drama/History/Romance
Year: 1963

Rating: Approved   Length: 192 minutes

Cast includes:

Elizabeth Taylor, Richard Burton, Rex Harrison, Pamela Brown, George Cole and more

And the Oscar goes to...

* Art Direction, John DeCuir, Jack Smith, Hilyard Brown, among others
* Cinematography, Leon Shamroy
* Costume Design, Irene Sharaff, Vittorio Novarese and Renie Conley
* Special Effects, Emil Kosa, Jr.

Brief movie overview

This is a historical epic tale of the triumphs and tragedy of the Egyptian queen, Cleopatra. Her beauty captivates Julius Caesar and Marc Antony, but Cleopatra loses in the end.

Caesar Chicken Wraps

½ C. Caesar salad dressing
½ C. grated Parmesan cheese, divided
1 tsp. lemon juice
1 clove garlic, minced
¼ tsp. pepper
1 (8 oz.) pkg. cream cheese, softened

3 C. shredded Romaine lettuce
½ C. diced sweet red pepper
1 (2¼ oz.) sliced black olives, drained
6 (10˝) flour tortillas
1¾ C. cooked, cubed chicken

In a small bowl, combine salad dressing, ¼ cup Parmesan cheese, lemon juice, garlic and pepper. In a small mixing bowl, beat cream cheese until smooth. Add half of the salad dressing mixture and mix well. Set aside. In a large bowl, combine lettuce, red pepper and olives. Add the remaining salad dressing mixture and toss to coat. Spread about ¼ cup of the cream cheese mixture onto each of the tortillas. Top with the lettuce mixture and chicken. Sprinkle with remaining Parmesan cheese.

Tom Jones

Movie Type: Adventure/Comedy/Romance
Year: 1963

Rating: Not Rated   Length: 128 minutes

Cast includes:

Albert Finney, Susannah York, Hugh Griffith, Edith Evans, Joan Greenwood and more

And the Oscar goes to…

☆ **Best Picture**
☆ **Best Director, Tony Richardson**
☆ **Best Music Score, John Addison**
☆ **Best Screenplay, John Osborne**

Brief movie overview

The love-'em-and-leave-'em lady charmer and son of a British country squire, Tom Jones, manages to come within moments of being hanged as a result of his mischief. Jones eventually finds his rightful place in life and love.

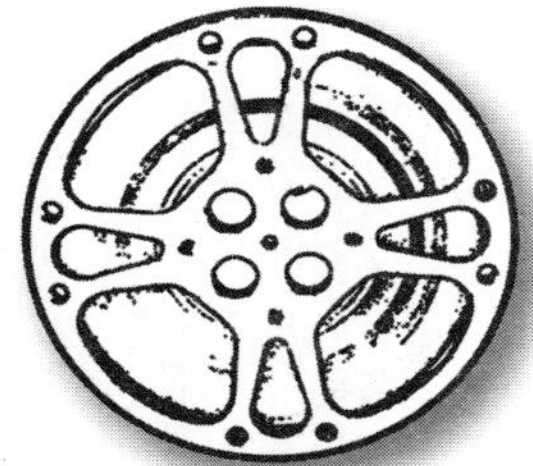

Fried Chicken

This classic meal staple is downed in one scene.

30 saltine crackers
2 T. flour
2 T. dry potato flakes
1 tsp. seasoned salt
½ tsp. pepper

1 egg
¼ C. vegetable oil
6 skinless, boneless
 chicken breast halves

Place crackers in a large resealable bag. Seal bag and crush crackers into coarse crumbs. Add flour, potato flakes, seasoned salt and pepper to bag and mix well. In a shallow dish, beat egg. Heat oil in a large skillet over medium-high heat. Dredge each chicken piece in egg then place in the bag with crumb mixture, seal and shake to coat. Reduce heat to medium and fry coated chicken, turning frequently, for 15 to 20 minutes or until golden brown and juices run clear.

Mary Poppins

Movie Type: Comedy/Drama/Musical/Fantasy
Year: 1964

Rating: G   Length: 140 minutes

Cast includes:

Julie Andrews, Dick Van Dyke, David Tomlinson and more

And the Oscar goes to...

* ☆ **Best Actress, Julie Andrews**
* ☆ **Film Editing, Cotton Warburton**
* ☆ **Best Music Score, Richard Sherman and Robert Sherman**
* ☆ **Best Song, "Chim Chim Cher-ee", music and lyrics by Richard Sherman and Robert Sherman**
* ☆ **Special Visual Effects, Peter Ellenshaw, Eustace Lycett and Hamilton Luske**

Brief movie overview

A magic nanny comes to work for a cold banker's unhappy family. The children's father grows increasingly disapproving of the assertive nanny's methods.

Poppy Seed Chicken

Vegetable oil

4 skinless, boneless chicken breast halves

1 (10½ oz.) can cream of chicken soup

1 (10½ oz.) can cream of mushroom soup

1 C. sour cream

1 (8 oz.) pkg. buttery round crackers, crushed

1 T. poppy seeds

½ C. butter, melted

In a large skillet over medium-high heat, heat oil. Reduce heat and cook chicken breasts, turning once until juices run clear and the chicken is no longer pink in the center. Set aside to cool. Preheat oven to 350°. Cut chicken into bite-size pieces. In a medium bowl, mix chicken pieces, soups and sour cream. Stir until well blended then transfer to a lightly greased 9 x 13″ baking dish. In another bowl, combine crushed crackers, poppy seeds and butter. Spread mixture evenly over chicken. Bake chicken for 30 minutes or until heated through and lightly browned on top.

The Lion in Winter

Movie Type: Drama
Year: 1968

Rating: PG   Length: 134 minutes

Cast includes:

Peter O'Toole, Katharine Hepburn, Anthony Hopkins, John Castle and more

And the Oscar goes to...

★ **Best Actress, Katharine Hepburn (tied with Barbra Streisand in Funny Girl)**
★ **Best Score, John Barry**
★ **Best Screenplay, James Goldman**

Brief movie overview

The three sons and scheming imprisoned wife of King Henry II all want to inherit the throne. With the fate of Henry's empire at stake, everybody engages in their own brand of deception and treachery to stake their claim.

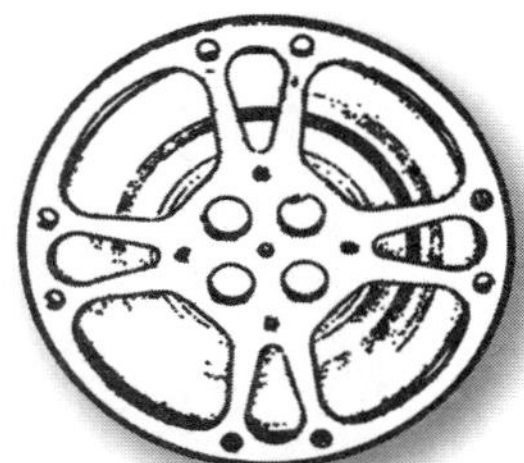

Barbecued Turkey Legs

A renaissance-themed dish makes a great accompaniment for this royal movie.

4 to 6 turkey legs
Salt and pepper to taste
¼ C. molasses
¼ C. cider vinegar
¼ C. ketchup

2 T. Worcestershire sauce
Dash of liquid smoke,
    optional
1 T. finely chopped onion

Preheat oven to 325°. Place turkey legs in lightly greased shallow baking dishes then sprinkle with salt and pepper. In a small bowl, combine molasses, cider vinegar, ketchup, Worcestershire sauce, liquid smoke and onion. Pour mixture over turkey legs. Bake for 1½ to 2 hours.

Movie Type: Adventure/Western/Drama
Year: 1969

Rating: G   Length: 128 minutes

Cast includes:

John Wayne, Glen Campbell, Kim Darby, Robert Duvall, Dennis Hopper and more

And the Oscar goes to...

☆ Best Actor, John Wayne

Brief movie overview

A young tomboy of a girl, Mattie Ross, sets to avenge her father's sudden death. She recruits a drunken, hard-nosed U.S. Marshal and a Texas Ranger to help. They set out from Arkansas into the Indian Territory.

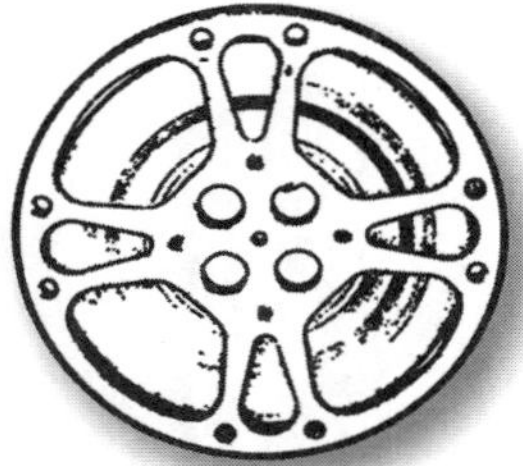

Baked Beef Stew

2 lbs. beef stew meat,
  cut into 1″ cubes
1 (14½ oz.) can diced
  tomatoes with juice
3 T. instant tapioca
1 T. beef bouillon granules
2 tsp. sugar
1½ tsp. salt

¼ tsp. pepper
4 carrots, cut into 1″ pieces
2 stalks celery,
  cut into ¾″ pieces
3 potatoes, peeled and cubed
1 onion, coarsely chopped
1 slice bread, cubed

Preheat oven to 375°. In a large skillet over medium heat, brown stew meat. Drain and set aside. In a large bowl, combine tomatoes in juice, 1 cup water, tapioca, beef bouillon granules, sugar, salt and pepper. Stir in browned beef, carrots, celery, potatoes, onion and bread cubes. Pour into a lightly greased 9 x 13″ baking dish. Cover and bake for 2 hours or until meat and vegetables are tender. Serve over baked biscuits.

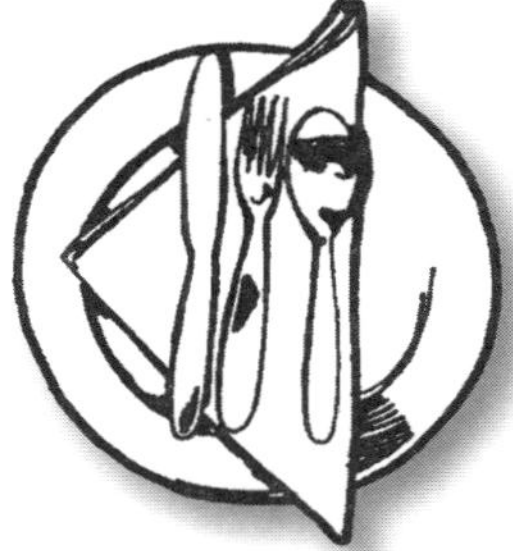

Love Story

Movie Type: Drama/Romance
Year: 1970

Rating: PG   Length: 99 minutes

Cast includes:

Ali MacGraw, Ryan O'Neal, John Marley, Ray Milland, Russel Nype and more

And the Oscar goes to...

★ Best Score, Francis Lai

Brief movie overview

Love means never having to say you're sorry... When a jock/Harvard Law student falls in love and decides to marry a Radcliffe music brain, his father threatens to disinherit him from the family will, leaving the young lovers to start their marriage at rock-bottom.

Grilled Peanut Butter & Jelly Sandwiches

PB&J's were often Oliver's lunch, brought to him by Jennifer while he was in law school.

Butter
8 slices bread

Peanut butter
Fruit jelly, any flavor

Place skillet over medium high heat. Spread butter on one side of each slice of bread. Spread peanut butter and jelly on unbuttered side of each slice. Place sandwiches, butter side down, in skillet. Brown sandwiches for 2 to 4 minutes on each side, or until golden brown and heated through.

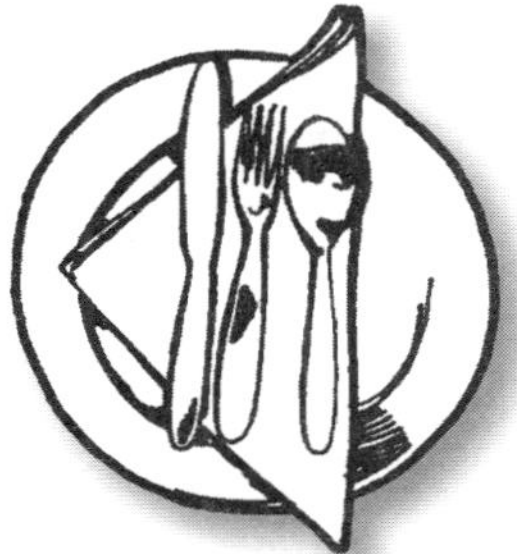

The Last Picture Show

Movie Type: Drama
Year: 1971

Rating: R   Length: 118 minutes

Cast includes:

Timothy Bottoms, Jeff Bridges, Cybill Shepherd, Ben Johnson and more

And the Oscar goes to...

☆ Best Supporting Actor, Ben Johnson
☆ Best Supporting Actress, Cloris Leachman

Brief movie overview

Enduring that awkward period of life between boyhood and manhood, best friends Sonny and Duane pass their time the best way they know how — with the movie house, basketball and girls. As high school graduation approaches, they learn some difficult lessons about love, loneliness and jealousy. Folks stop attending features at the movie house and the time comes for the last picture show.

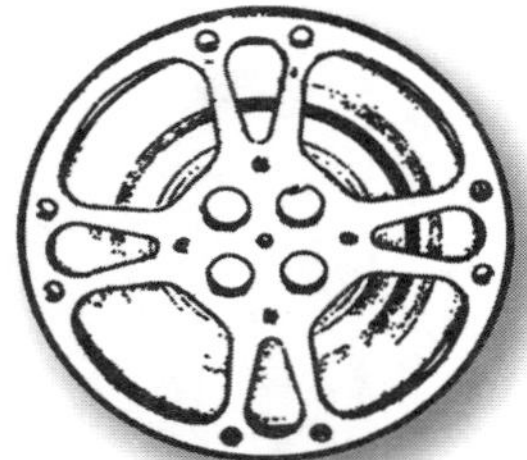

Cola Burgers

1 egg
½ C. cola, divided
½ C. crushed
  saltine crackers

6 T. French salad
  dressing, divided
2 T. grated Parmesan cheese
1½ lbs. ground beef

Preheat grill to high heat. Once grill is hot, lightly oil grate. In a medium bowl, mix egg, ¼ cup cola, cracker crumbs, 2 tablespoons French dressing and Parmesan cheese. Crumble ground beef into the mixture and mix by hand until well blended. Form mixture into six ¾″ thick patties. In a small bowl, combine remaining cola and dressing. Grill burgers for approximately 3 minutes on each side. Brush with the dressing mixture then grill for 8 to 10 additional minutes, basting occasionally.

The Godfather

Movie Type: Crime/Drama
Year: 1972

Rating: R   Length: 175 minutes

Cast includes:

Marlon Brando, Al Pacino, James Caan, Robert Duvall and more

And the Oscar goes to...

☆ **Best Picture**
☆ **Best Actor, Marlon Brando**
☆ **Best Screenplay, Mario Puzo and Francis Coppola**

Brief movie overview

The aging patriarch of an organized crime dynasty, Don Vito Corleone, transfers control of his clandestine empire to his beloved but reluctant son, Michael.

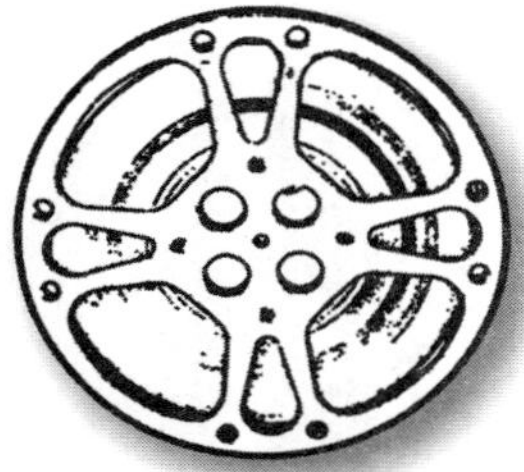

Authentic Spaghetti and Meatballs

1½ T. olive oil

6 T. chopped onion

2 cloves garlic, minced

1 (16 oz.) can crushed tomatoes

1-½ (6 oz.) cans tomato paste

¼ C. sugar

2 T. chopped fresh oregano, divided

1 dried bay leaf

Salt and pepper to taste

½ lb. ground beef

¼ C. Italian seasoned bread crumbs

2 T. chopped fresh parsley

1 egg, lightly beaten

¼ C. grated Parmesan cheese

½ (16 oz.) pkg. uncooked spaghetti

In a large saucepan over medium heat, heat olive oil then add onion and cook until lightly browned. Mix in garlic and cook for 1 additional minute. Stir in crushed tomatoes, tomato paste, ½ cup water, sugar, 1 tablespoon oregano, bay leaf, salt and pepper. Bring to a boil then reduce heat to low and simmer while preparing meatballs. In a large bowl, mix ground beef, bread crumbs, parsley, egg and cheese. Season with salt and pepper. Roll mixture into 1″ balls and drop into sauce. Cook for 40 minutes or until the internal temperature of the meatballs reaches 160°. In a large pot, bring lightly salted water to a boil. Stir in spaghetti. Cook for 8 to 10 minutes until al dente then drain. Serve meatballs and sauce over cooked spaghetti.

Cabaret

Movie Type: Drama/Musical
Year: 1972

Rating: PG   Length: 124 minutes

Cast includes:

Liza Minnelli, Michael York, Helmut Griem, Joel Grey, Fritz Wepper and more

And the Oscar goes to...

* Best Actress, Liza Minnelli
* Best Supporting Actor, Joel Grey
* Best Director, Bob Fosse
* Also won for Art Direction, Cinematography, Film Editing, Music Score and Sound

Brief movie overview

Sally Bowles, an American singer at the Kit-Kat club in 1930s Berlin, romances two men while the Nazi Party rises to power around them.

Kraut Bierocks

1½ (¼ oz.) pkgs.
    active dry yeast
½ C. sugar
4 C. flour
½ C. powdered milk
1½ tsp. baking powder
½ C. shortening
1 lb. lean ground beef
1 lb. ground Italian sausage

1 C. chopped onion
3 C. shredded cabbage
3 T. mustard
2 tsp. salt
2 tsp. pepper
½ C. shredded, processed
    American cheese
½ C. shredded
    Cheddar cheese

In a medium bowl, combine yeast, sugar and 2 cups water. Mix until well blended then let stand for 10 minutes. Stir in flour, powdered milk, baking powder and shortening. Then knead mixture for 10 minutes, adding flour as necessary. Cover bowl with a damp cloth and let rise in a warm place for 30 minutes then knead again. Meanwhile, in a large skillet, over medium-high heat, brown beef, sausage and onion. Drain excess fat from skillet then stir in cabbage, mustard, salt and pepper. Cook for 5 minutes. Add cheeses and heat, stirring until cheese is melted. Preheat oven to 350°. Separate dough into 10 pieces. Flatten each piece and place a large spoonful of meat filling in the center of each. Fold over to form a round bun. Lay each with the folded side down on a lightly greased 9 x 13″ baking dish. Bake for 20 minutes or until golden brown.

One Flew over the Cuckoo's Nest

Movie Type: Drama
Year: 1975

Rating: R   Length: 133 minutes

Cast includes:

Jack Nicholson, Louise Fletcher, William Redfield, Michael Berryman and more

And the Oscar goes to...

☆ **Best Picture**
☆ **Best Actor, Jack Nicholson**
☆ **Best Actress, Louise Fletcher**
☆ **Best Director, Milos Forman**
☆ **Best Screenplay, Lawrence Hauben and Bo Goldman**

Brief movie overview

McMurphy thinks he can get out of doing work while in prison by pretending to be mad, though his plan backfires when he is sent to a mental asylum. The tale ensues as McMurphy tries to liven up the asylum by playing with his fellow inmates, but the oppressive Nurse Ratched is after him.

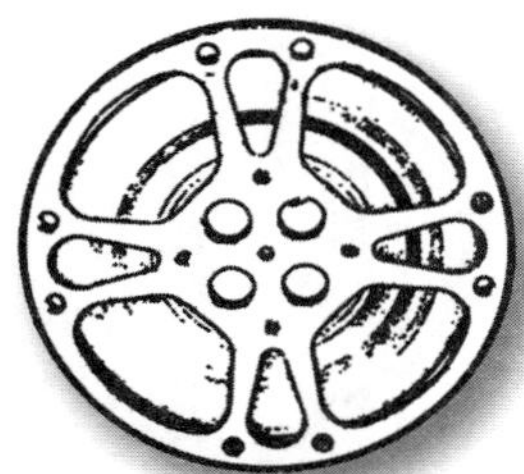

"Lost Your Noodle" Tuna Casserole

1 (8 oz.) pkg. uncooked medium egg noodles
½ C. butter, divided
½ medium onion, finely chopped
1 stalk celery, finely chopped
1 clove garlic, minced
1 (8 oz.) pkg. button mushrooms, sliced

¼ C. flour
2 C. milk
Salt and pepper to taste
2 (6 oz.) cans tuna, drained and flaked
1 C. frozen peas, thawed
3 T. bread crumbs
2 T. butter, melted
1 C. shredded Cheddar cheese

Preheat oven to 375°. Bring a large pot of lightly salted water to a boil. Add egg noodles and cook for 8 to 10 minutes, until al dente, and drain. In a skillet, over medium-low heat, melt 1 tablespoon butter. Mix in onion, celery and garlic, and cook for 5 minutes. Increase heat to medium-high and add mushrooms. Continue to cook, stirring occasionally, for 5 minutes or until most of the liquid has evaporated. In a medium saucepan, melt 4 tablespoons butter. Whisk in flour until smooth. Gradually whisk in milk and continue cooking for 5 minutes, until sauce is smooth and slightly thickened. Season with salt and pepper. Add tuna, peas, mushroom mixture and cooked noodles. Mix well. Grease a 9 x 13″ baking dish with 1 tablespoon butter and transfer mixture into baking dish. In a small bowl, melt remaining 2 tablespoons of butter and mix with bread crumbs. Sprinkle over casserole. Top with cheese and bake for 25 minutes or until bubbly and lightly browned.

Rocky

Movie Type: Action/Drama/Romance
Year: 1976

Rating: PG   Length: 119 minutes

Cast includes:

Sylvester Stallone, Talia Shire, Burt Young, Carl Weathers, Burgess Meredith and more

And the Oscar goes to...

☆ **Best Picture**
☆ **Best Director, John Avildsen**
☆ **Film Editing, Richard Halsey and Scott Conrad**

Brief movie overview

A small time boxer, Rocky Balboa, gets a once-in-a-lifetime chance to fight the heavyweight champ when Apollo Creed visits Philadelphia. Creed's managers want to set up an exhibition match, touting the fight as a chance for a "nobody" to become a "somebody".

Philly Cheese Steaks

6 T. oil, divided
1 large Spanish onion, diced
24 oz. thin-sliced
  ribeye steak
Cheese (Cheez Whiz,
  American or Provolone)
4 crusty Italian rolls

Sweet green and red peppers
  sautéed in oil, optional
Mushrooms sautéed
  in oil, optional

In a medium skillet over medium heat, add 3 tablespoons oil to the pan and sauté onions to desired doneness. Remove onions and set aside. Add remaining oil and quickly sauté steak on each side. If necessary, melt cheese over double boiler or in microwave. Divide meat among 4 rolls. Add onions, any additional desired toppings and pour cheese over filling.

Annie Hall

Movie Type: Comedy/Romance
Year: 1977

Rating: PG   Length: 93 minutes

Cast includes:

Woody Allen, Diane Keaton, Tony Roberts, Carol Kane, Paul Simon and more

And the Oscar goes to…

☆ Best Picture
☆ Best Actress, Diane Keaton
☆ Best Director, Woody Allen
☆ Best Screenplay, Woody Allen and Marshall Brickman

Brief movie overview

A historical document about love in the 1970s, told through the romantic adventures of a neurotic New York comedian, Alvy Singer, and his equally neurotic girlfriend, Annie Hall.

Lobster Bisque

6 T. butter
6 T. flour
1 tsp. salt
¼ tsp. pepper
½ tsp. celery salt
4½ C. milk

1½ C. chicken broth
3 T. minced onion
3 C. cooked lobster meat, shredded
1 T. paprika
½ C. light cream

In a large pot over medium heat, melt butter. Stir in flour, salt, pepper and celery salt. Mix until well blended. Gradually stir in milk, being careful that lumps do not form, then stir in chicken broth. Cook over low heat, stirring constantly, until the soup begins to thicken. Add onion, lobster and paprika. Continue to cook and stir for an additional 10 minutes. Stir in cream, and heat thoroughly before serving.

Close Encounters of the Third Kind

Movie Type: Adventure/Drama/Sci-Fi
Year: 1977

Rating: PG   Length: 132 minutes

Cast includes:

Richard Dreyfuss, Francois Truffaut, Teri Garr, Melinda Dillon and more

And the Oscar goes to...

☆ **Cinematography, Vilmos Zsigmond**
☆ **Sound Effects Editing, Frank Warner**

Brief movie overview

A line worker, Roy Neary, sets out to investigate a power outage when his truck stalls and he is bathed in light from above. After this, strange visions and five musical notes keep running through his mind and he feels undeniably drawn to an isolated area in the wilderness.

Meat Gravy over Mountain Potatoes

6 potatoes, peeled
   and cubed
Milk
Butter
2 lbs. lean ground beef

1 small onion, diced
¼ C. flour
1 qt. milk
1 tsp. onion salt
Salt and pepper to taste

Place potatoes in a large pot of lightly salted boiling water. Cook until tender then mash with milk and butter until desired consistency has been reached. Set aside. In a large, deep skillet, place ground beef and onion. Crumble and cook over medium-high heat until evenly browned. Remove from heat and sprinkle flour over cooked mixture. Stir until evenly coated and all liquid is absorbed. Place skillet over medium heat, add half of the milk and stir until gravy begins to thicken. Add remaining milk until desired consistency has been reached and bring gravy to a boil. Season with onion salt, salt and pepper. Mound up potatoes on each plate like a mountain. Spoon meat mixture over mashed potatoes and serve.

Chariots of Fire

Movie Type: Drama/History
Year: 1981

Rating: PG   **Length:** 123 minutes

Cast includes:

Nicholas Farrell, Nigel Havers, Ian Charleson, Ben Cross and more

And the Oscar goes to...

☆ Best Picture
☆ Costume Design, Milena Canonero
☆ Best Score, Vangelis
☆ Best Screenplay, Colin Welland

Brief movie overview

The true story of two British track athletes competing in the 1924 Summer Olympic Games. One is a devout Scottish missionary who runs for God, the other is a Jewish student at Cambridge who runs for fame and to escape prejudice.

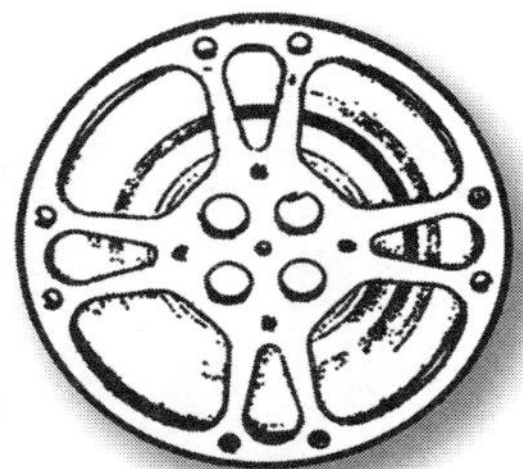

Baked Pork Chops

A delicious dish that is served up in one scene.

6 pork chops
1 tsp. garlic powder
1 tsp. seasoning salt
2 eggs, beaten
¼ C. flour
2 C. Italian-style seasoned
   bread crumbs

4 T. olive oil
1 (10¾ oz.) can cream
   of mushroom soup
½ C. milk
⅓ C. white wine

Preheat oven to 350°. Season pork chops with garlic powder and seasoning salt. Place beaten eggs, flour and bread crumbs in 3 separate shallow bowls. Dredge chops in flour, dip in egg then coat generously with bread crumbs. In a medium skillet over medium-high heat, heat oil. Fry the pork chops for 5 minutes on each side or until breading is browned. Transfer chops to a lightly greased 9 x 13″ baking dish. Cover with foil. Bake for 1 hour. Combine soup, milk and white wine. After pork chops have baked for 1 hour, remove from oven and pour soup mixture over all. Cover and bake for an additional 30 minutes.

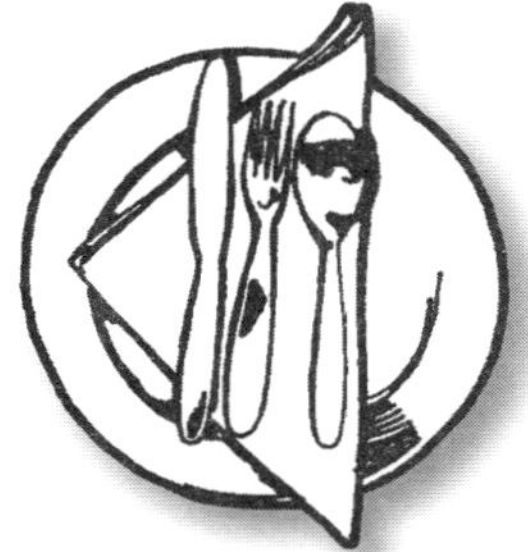

E.T. The Extra-Terrestrial

Movie Type: Drama/Fastasy/Sci-Fi

Year: 1982

Rating: PG

Length: 120 minutes

Cast includes:

Henry Thomas, Dee Wallace-Stone, Robert MacNaughton, Drew Barrymore, Peter Coyote and more

And the Oscar goes to...

☆ **Best Score, John Williams**

☆ **Best Sound, Robert Knudson, Robert Glass, among others**

☆ **Sound Effects Editing, Charles Campbell and Ben Burtt**

☆ **Visual Effects, Carlo Rambaldi, Dennis Muren and Kenneth Smith**

Brief movie overview

A group of children help a stranded alien return home, but members of the task force are working day and night to track down the whereabouts of Earth's first visitor from outer space.

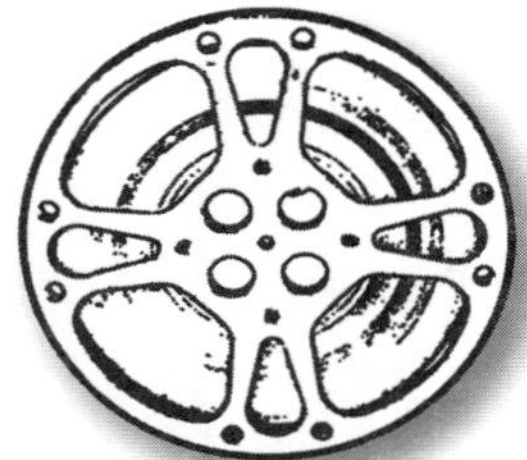

Out of This World Friendship Soup

1 lb. ground beef
Pepper to taste
Fresh minced garlic to taste
1 (14½ oz.) can diced tomatoes
1 (6 oz.) can tomato paste
½ C. dried split peas
⅓ C. beef bouillon granules

¼ C. pearl barley
½ C. dried lentils
¼ C. dried onion flakes
2 tsp. Italian seasoning
¼ C. long-grain white rice
2 bay leaves
½ C. small pasta

In a large pot over medium heat, crumble and brown ground beef with pepper and garlic. Drain excess fat. Add diced tomatoes, tomato paste, 12 cups water, peas, bouillon, barley, lentils, onion flakes, Italian seasoning, rice and bay leaves. Bring to a boil then reduce to a simmer. Continue to simmer for 45 minutes. Stir in pasta, cover and simmer for an additional 15 to 20 minutes or until the pasta, peas, lentils and barley are tender.

Tootsie

Movie Type: Comedy/Romance
Year: 1982

Rating: PG   Length: 119 minutes

Cast includes:

Dustin Hoffman, Jessica Lange, Teri Garr, Dabney Coleman, Bill Murray and more

And the Oscar goes to...

☆ Best Supporting Actress, Jessica Lange

Brief movie overview

Michael Dorsey, an unemployed actor, is desperate for work and has a reputation of being difficult. He disguises himself and lands the role of a female soap opera star. The plots thickens as Dorsey falls for another actress, but she, and everyone else, still think he's a woman.

Imitation Crab Quiche

2 eggs, beaten
½ C. milk
½ C. mayonnaise or
  sour cream
1 tsp. cornstarch
1½ C. shredded
  Swiss cheese

½ lb. imitation crabmeat
1 pinch pepper
1 (9″) prepared deep
  dish pie shell

Preheat oven to 350°. In a medium bowl, combine eggs, milk, mayonnaise and cornstarch. Stir in cheese, crab and pepper. Pour into prepared pie shell. Bake for 35 to 40 minutes or until a knife inserted in the center comes out clean. Cool slightly before serving.

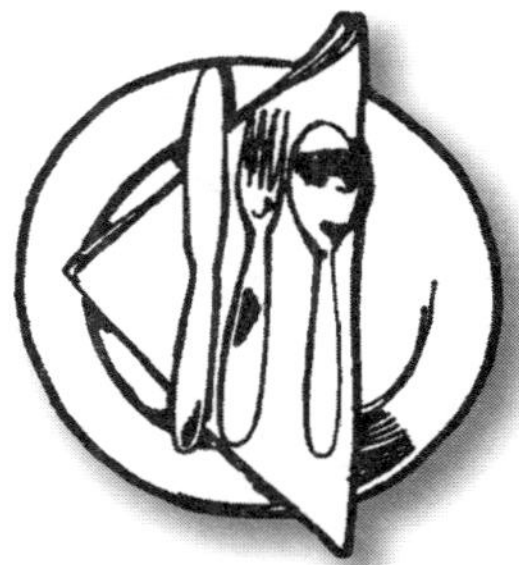

Terms of Endearment

Movie Type: Romance/Comedy/Drama
Year: 1983

Rating: PG   Length: 132 minutes

Cast includes:

Shirley MacLaine, Debra Winger, Jack Nicholson, Danny DeVito and more

And the Oscar goes to...

☆ **Best Picture**
☆ **Best Actress, Shirley MacLaine**
☆ **Best Supporting Actor, Jack Nicholson**
☆ **Best Director, James Brooks**
☆ **Best Screenplay, James Brooks**

Brief movie overview

Mother and daughter, Aurora and Emma, march to the beat of very different drummers and each shows their love in very different ways. The tale covers several years of their lives, as each find different reasons to go on living and find joy.

Love My Sweet Honey Chicken Kabobs

¼ C. vegetable oil
⅓ C. honey
⅓ C. soy sauce
¼ tsp. pepper
8 skinless, boneless
   chicken breast halves,
   cut into 1″ cubes

2 cloves garlic
5 small onions,
   cut into 2″ pieces
2 red bell peppers,
   cut into 2″ pieces
Skewers

In a large bowl, whisk together oil, honey, soy sauce and pepper. Reserve a small amount of marinade for basting. Place chicken cubes, garlic, onions and peppers in the large bowl, and marinate in the refrigerator for at least 2 hours. Preheat the grill at high heat. Drain marinade from chicken and vegetables, and discard marinade. Alternately skewer chicken cubes and vegetables. Lightly oil grill grate, and place skewers on grill. Cook for 12 to 15 minutes or until chicken is cooked through, frequently turning and basting with reserved marinade.

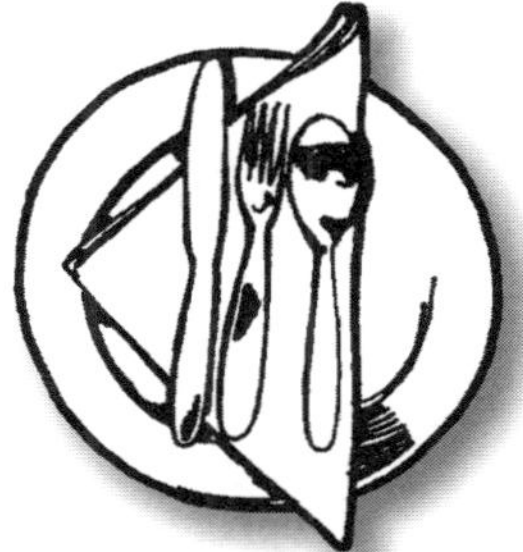

Moonstruck

Movie Type: Comedy/Romance/Drama
Year: 1987

Rating: PG   Length: 102 minutes

Cast includes:

Cher, Nicolas Cage, Vincent Gardenia, Olympia Dukakis, Danny Aiello and more

And the Oscar goes to...

☆ **Best Actress, Cher**
☆ **Best Supporting Actress, Olympia Dukakis**
☆ **Best Screenplay, John Shanley**

Brief movie overview

A widowed Brooklyn bookkeeper, Loretta Castorini, is convinced that marrying Johnny Cammareri is the safe and sure thing to do, though she admits to her mother that she's not really in love with Johnny. Complications occur when Loretta meets Johnny's estranged, moody and passionate younger brother, Ronny.

Easy Three Cheese Pepperoni Pizza

1 (12″) pre-baked
   pizza crust or crust
   of your choice
Olive oil
1 C. pizza sauce
½ C. shredded
   Cheddar cheese

½ C. shredded
   mozzarella cheese
¼ C. crumbled feta cheese
1 (3½ oz.) pkg.
   pepperoni slices

Preheat oven to 450°. Place pre-baked pizza crust directly on oven rack for 2 to 3 minutes, remove crust from oven and brush with a thin layer of olive oil. Spread pizza sauce evenly over crust. Layer shredded Cheddar cheese, shredded mozzarella cheese and crumbled feta cheese evenly over the sauce. Arrange pepperoni slices over cheese on pizza. Reduce oven temperature to 425°. Bake pizza directly on oven rack for 8 to 10 minutes, or until cheese melts. Remove pizza from oven and let cool 5 minutes before cutting into slices and serving.

Beetle Juice

Movie Type: Comedy/Fantasy/Horror
Year: 1988

Rating: PG   Length: 92 minutes

Cast includes:

Winona Ryder, Michael Keaton, Alec Baldwin, Geena Davis and more

And the Oscar goes to...

☆ **Best Make-Up, Ve Neill, Steve La Porte and Robert Short**

Brief movie overview

After their attempts to scare off the yuppie family that has moved into their New England farmhouse fail, the ghosts of Barbara and Adam Maitland turn to another ghost for help, Beetlejuice – the self-proclaimed "bio-exorcist".

Grilled Shrimp Skewers

Watch out! These shrimp may come to life during the dinner scene!

3 cloves garlic, minced
⅓ C. olive oil
¼ C. tomato sauce
2 T. red wine vinegar
2 T. chopped fresh basil

½ tsp. salt
¼ tsp. cayenne pepper
2 lbs. fresh shrimp,
   peeled and deveined
Skewers

In a large bowl, combine garlic, olive oil, tomato sauce and vinegar. Stir in basil, salt and cayenne pepper. Add shrimp to marinade and stir until shrimp are evenly coated. Cover and refrigerate for 30 minutes to 1 hour, stirring occasionally. Preheat grill to medium heat. Skewer shrimp by piercing once by the tail and again near the head. Discard marinade. Lightly oil grill grate. Grill for 2 to 3 minutes on each side until shrimp are opaque.

A Fish Called Wanda

Movie Type: Comedy/Crime
Year: 1988

Rating: R   Length: 108 minutes

Cast includes:

John Cleese, Jamie Lee Curtis, Kevin Kline, Michael Palin, Maria Aitken and more

And the Oscar goes to...

☆ Best Supporting Actor, Kevin Kline

Brief movie overview

Four very different characters team up to commit armed robbery in London. The story continues as they all try to double cross each other for the loot.

Fish & Chips

½ C. flour
½ C. cornmeal
¼ tsp. salt
4 to 6 oz. beer

4 C. vegetable oil for frying
4 large russet potatoes
2 lbs. fish fillets, cut in half, crosswise

Preheat oven to 250°. In a shallow bowl, combine flour, cornmeal and salt. Add beer and mix until well combined. Batter should be thin. Peel and cut potatoes into finger-sized pieces. Heat oil in deep fryer. Cook a third of the potatoes until golden brown. Drain on paper towels and place in warm oven. Repeat with remaining potatoes. Dredge fillets in batter allowing excess to drip off. Fry fish in several batches for 5 to 8 minutes or until golden brown and fish flakes easily with a fork. Drain on paper towels and place in warm oven until all fish are done.

Rain Man

Movie Type: Adventure/Comedy/Drama
Year: 1988

Rating: R   Length: 133 minutes

Cast includes:

Dustin Hoffman, Tom Cruise, Valeria Golino, Gerald Molen, Jack Murdock and more

And the Oscar goes to...

☆ **Best Picture**
☆ **Best Actor, Dustin Hoffman**
☆ **Best Director, Barry Levinson**
☆ **Best Screenplay, Ronald Bass and Barry Morrow**

Brief movie overview

Charlie Babbitt believes he is entitled to a fortune after his father dies. But his father left him something else — a now antique convertible and an unknown autistic brother, Raymond, who is the true owner of their father's fortune. The two brothers begin a long road trip that will lead them to an understanding of each other.

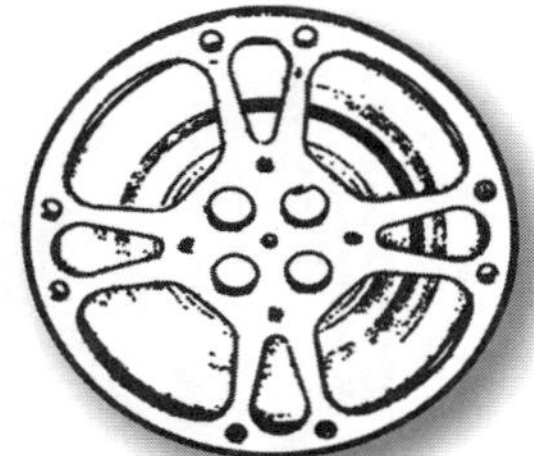

Casino Clams

24 small clams in shell
Salt to taste
¼ C. butter, softened
¼ C. chopped green onion
¼ C. finely chopped green
   bell pepper

¼ C. finely chopped celery
1 T. lemon juice
4 slices bacon, cooked
   until crisp and crumbled
Rock salt

Preheat oven to 425°. Open clams and remove from shell. Wash shells then place each clam in the deep half of the shell. Discard remaining clam shell halves. Season each clam with a little salt. In a medium bowl, blend butter, chopped green onion, chopped bell pepper, chopped celery, lemon juice, and crumbled bacon. Top each clam with ¾ tablespoon of the vegetable mixture. Arrange the clam shells on a bed of rock salt in a shallow baking pan. Bake for 10 to 12 minutes.

Batman

Movie Type: Action/Crime/Fantasy/Thriller
Year: 1989

Rating: PG-13   Length: 126 minutes

Cast includes:

Michael Keaton, Jack Nicholson, Kim Basinger, Robert Wuhl and more

And the Oscar goes to...

☆ Art Direction, Anton Furst and Peter Young

Brief movie overview

Batman, the dark knight of Gotham City, begins his war on crime with his first major enemy being the clownishly homicidal Joker.

Kickin' Wings

1 C. butter
1 C. hot sauce
4 dashes pepper
4 dashes garlic
  powder
2 C. flour

1 tsp. paprika
1 tsp. cayenne pepper
1 tsp. salt
40 chicken wings
Oil for deep frying

In a small saucepan over low heat, combine butter, hot sauce, pepper and garlic powder, stirring until butter is melted. Remove from heat and set aside. In a small bowl, mix flour, paprika, cayenne pepper and salt. Place wings in a large glass dish and sprinkle flour mixture over them until evenly coated. Cover and refrigerate for 60 to 90 minutes. Heat oil in deep fryer to 375°. Fry wings in hot oil for 10 to 15 minutes or until parts of wings begin to turn brown. Remove from heat. In a serving bowl, combine wings and hot sauce mixture.

Dances With Wolves

Movie Type: Adventure/Drama/History
Year: 1990

Rating: PG-13   Length: 224 minutes

Cast includes:

Kevin Costner, Mary McDonnell, Graham Greene, Rodney Grant and more

And the Oscar goes to...

☆ **Best Picture**
☆ **Best Director, Kevin Costner**
☆**Also won for Cinematography, Film Editing, Best Score and Sound**

Brief movie overview

Lt. John Dunbar, an accidental military hero, requests a position on the deserted western front. He soon finds that he is not alone as he encounters a wolf and a curious Indian tribe. His friendship with the tribe and wolves make him an intolerable aberration in the military.

Winter Corn Chowder

1½ C. dried corn
3 C. chicken broth
6 slices bacon
2 C. chopped onion

4 C. milk
2 tsp. sugar
½ tsp. salt

Rinse corn. In a large saucepan, combine corn and broth. Bring to a boil. Remove from heat and allow to stand for 2 hours. Heat mixture once again and simmer for 45 minutes. Fry bacon in a skillet until crisp. Drain and set aside. In bacon drippings, sauté onion. Add onions to corn mixture and simmer for an additional 5 minutes. Stir in milk, sugar and salt. Heat through and serve.

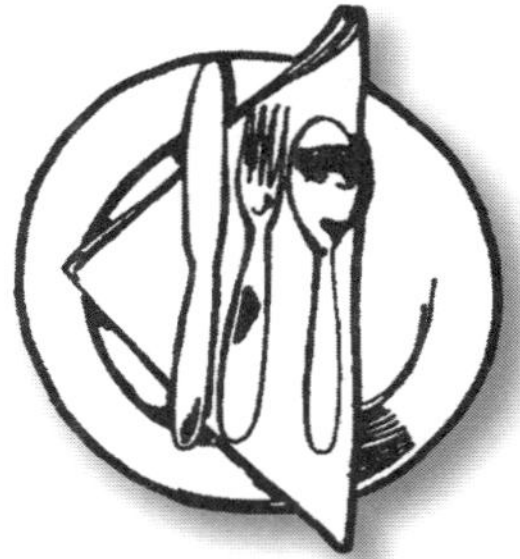

City Slickers

Movie Type: Adventure/Comedy/Western
Year: 1991

Rating: PG-13   Length: 112 minutes

Cast includes:

Billy Crystal, Daniel Stern, Bruno Kirby, Patricia Wettig, Helen Slater, Jack Palance and more

And the Oscar goes to…

☆ Best Supporting Actor, Jack Palance

Brief movie overview

Mitch, a big-city radio ad salesman, is plagued with a mid-life crisis, along with his friends Ed and Phil. The men find renewal and purpose on a cattle driving vacation.

Cowboy Chili

1 lb. lean ground beef	1 T. chili powder
1 medium onion, chopped	¾ tsp. salt
2 cloves garlic, minced	1 (15 oz.) can chili beans
½ C. tomato sauce	2 T. green pepper sauce
½ C. water	

In a large skillet over medium heat, crumble and brown ground beef for 5 minutes. Add onion and garlic, and cook, stirring often, for 5 additional minutes or until tender. Drain excess fat. Stir in tomato sauce, water, chili powder and salt. Mix until well blended. Bring to a boil then reduce heat, and simmer for 5 minutes or until most of the liquid has evaporated. Stir in chili beans and green pepper sauce. Thoroughly heat and serve.

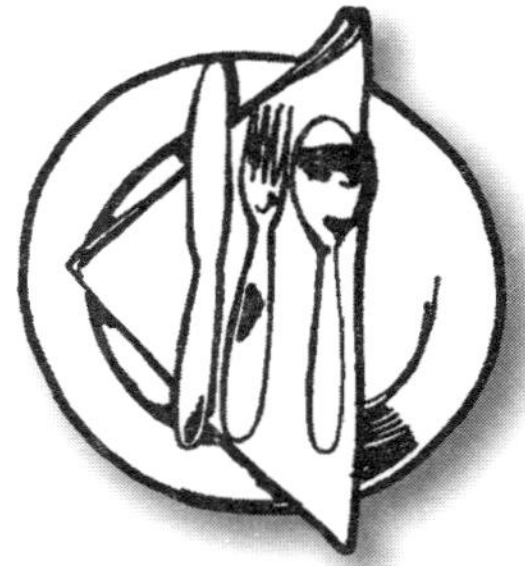

Mrs. Doubtfire

Movie Type: Comedy/Drama
Year: 1993

Rating: PG-13   Length: 125 minutes

Cast includes:

Robin Williams, Sally Field, Pierce Brosnan and more

And the Oscar goes to...

☆ Best Make-Up, Greg Cannom, Ve Neill and Yolanda Toussieng

Brief movie overview

After a bitter divorce, an actor disguises himself as a female housekeeper, Mrs. Doubtfire, in order to spend secret time with his children held in custody by his ex-wife.

Spicy Shrimp Creole

1½ T. vegetable oil
1 C. julienne celery
1 onion, chopped
2 cloves garlic, crushed
½ tsp. sugar
1 T. flour
½ tsp. salt
½ tsp. pepper

¼ tsp. cayenne pepper
1 (14½ oz.) can
  crushed tomatoes
½ (15 oz.) can tomato sauce
½ bay leaf
½ T. hot pepper sauce
1 lb. medium shrimp,
  peeled and deveined

In a large pot over medium heat, heat oil. Sauté celery, onions and garlic until the onions are almost translucent. Add sugar, flour, salt, pepper and cayenne pepper and mix well. Mix in crushed tomatoes, tomato sauce, bay leaf and hot sauce. Bring mixture to a boil then reduce heat and simmer for 30 minutes, stirring occasionally. Stir shrimp into mixture approximately 15 minutes before serving. May need to raise temperature to ensure mixture is bubbling, but not burning. Remove bay leaf and serve once shrimp are pink and thoroughly cooked.

The Piano

Movie Type: Drama/Romance
Year: 1993

Rating: R   Length: 121 minutes

Cast includes:

Holly Hunter, Harvey Keitel, Sam Neill, Anna Paquin, Kerry Walker and more

And the Oscar goes to...

☆ **Best Actress, Holly Hunter**
☆ **Best Supporting Actress, Anna Paquin**
☆ **Best Screenplay, Jane Campion**

Brief movie overview

Ada, a mute, is sent to mid-nineteenth century New Zealand's South Island for an arranged marriage. She leaves her native Scotland accompanied by her daughter, Flora, and her beloved piano. Life in the rugged forests is not all she had imagined and neither is her relationship with her new husband Stewart.

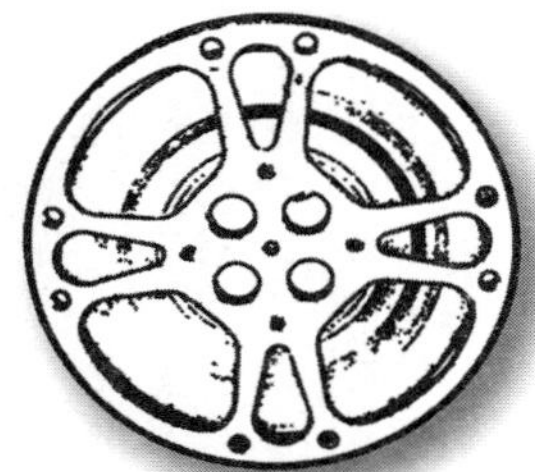

Chicken Fingers

1 egg, beaten
1 C. buttermilk
1½ tsp. garlic powder
6 skinless, boneless
   chicken breast halves,
   cut into ½″ strips

1 C. flour
1 C. seasoned bread crumbs
1 tsp. salt
1 tsp. baking powder
1 qt. oil for frying

In a small bowl, mix the egg, buttermilk and garlic powder. Place the egg mixture and chicken pieces in a large resealable bag. Seal bag, and refrigerate for 2 to 4 hours. In another large, resealable bag, mix together flour, bread crumbs, salt and baking powder. Remove chicken from refrigerator and drain and discard egg mixture. Place chicken in the bag of flour, seal and shake to completely coat chicken. In a large, heavy skillet, heat oil to 375°. Using tongs, carefully place coated chicken strips in hot oil. Fry until golden brown and chicken juices run clear. Drain on paper towels and serve.

Forrest Gump

Movie Type: Comedy/Drama
Year: 1994

Rating: PG-13   Length: 142 minutes

Cast includes:

Tom Hanks, Gary Sinise, Robin Wright Penn, Sally Field, Mykelti Williamson and more

And the Oscar goes to...

☆ **Best Picture**
☆ **Best Actor, Tom Hanks**
☆ **Best Director, Robert Zemickis**

Brief movie overview

A low-intelligence man tells his life's tale to people waiting at a small town bus stop. He has captured fame, fortune and glory, but his one true love has continuously eluded him.

Shrimp Gumbo

Makes 4 servings

4 T. vegetable oil, divided
2 T. flour
2 lbs. medium shrimp, peeled and de-veined
3 C. chopped okra
2 onions, chopped
1 (14½ oz.) can diced tomatoes

2 qts. water
1 bay leaf
3 cloves garlic, minced
1 tsp. salt
1 red bell pepper, chopped
Pepper to taste

In a large skillet over high heat, place 2 tablespoons vegetable oil and flour. Whisk together quickly until combined. Continue to heat, stirring constantly, until a dark roux forms. Stir in peeled shrimp and heat for 2 to 3 minutes, until shrimp turn pink. Remove from skillet and set aside. In a separate skillet, heat remaining 2 tablespoons vegetable oil. Stir in chopped okra and chopped onions, heating until okra is tender. Stir in diced tomatoes and add water, bay leaf, garlic, salt, chopped red pepper and prepared shrimp mixture. Toss together well and heat for an additional 30 minutes.

The Lion King

Movie Type: Animation/Adventure/Comedy/Drama
Year: 1994

Rating: G   Length: 89 minutes

Voices for Cast includes:

Jonathan Taylor Thomas, Matthew Broderick, James Earl Jones, Moira Kelly, Whoopi Goldberg and more

And the Oscar goes to...

☆ **Best Score, Hans Zimmer**
☆ **Best Song, "Can You Feel the Love Tonight",**
  music by Elton John, lyrics by Tim Rice

Brief movie overview

Tricked into thinking he killed his father, a guilt-ridden lion cub flees into exile and abandons his identity as the future King.

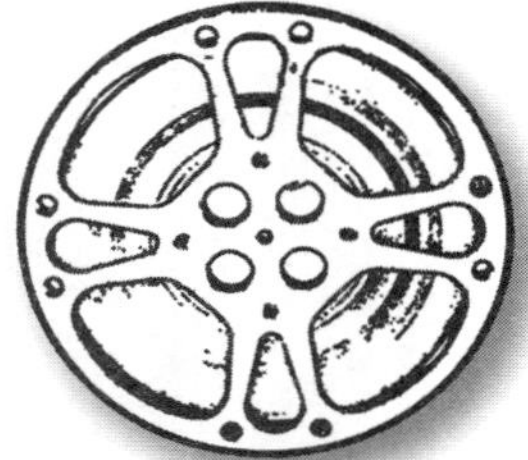

Ham & Pineapple Kabobs

"What do you want me to do, dress in drag and do the hula?" Timon

3 T. brown sugar
2 T. distilled white vinegar
1 T. vegetable oil
1 tsp. prepared mustard
¾ lb. cooked ham,
   cut into 1″ cubes

1 (15 oz.) can pineapple
   chunks, drained
Skewers

Preheat grill for high heat. In a medium bowl, mix brown sugar, vinegar, vegetable oil and mustard until well blended. Thread ham and pineapple chunks alternately onto skewers. Lightly oil the grill grate. Place kabobs on grill, and brush generously with the brown sugar baste. Cook for 6 to 8 minutes, turning frequently and basting often. Serve when heated thoroughly and well-glazed.

Braveheart

Movie Type: Action/Drama/History
Year: 1995

Rating: R   Length: 177 minutes

Cast includes:

Mel Gibson, James Robinson, Sean Lawlor, Sandy Nelson, James Cosmo and more

And the Oscar goes to...

☆ **Best Picture**
☆ **Best Director, Mel Gibson**
☆ **Also won for Cinematography, Best Make-Up, Sound Effects Editing**

Brief movie overview

A Scottish rebel, William Wallace, leads an uprising against the cruel English ruler who wishes to inherit the crown of Scotland. When he was a young boy, Wallace's father and brother lost their lives trying to free Scotland, along with many others.

Lamb Stew

1 T. olive oil

2 lbs. boneless lamb shoulder, cut into 1½″ pieces

½ tsp. salt

Pepper to taste

1 large onion, sliced

2 carrots, peeled and cut into large chunks

1 parsnip, peeled and cut into large chunks, optional

4 C. water, more if needed

3 large potatoes, peeled and quartered

1 C. coarsely chopped leeks

1 T. chopped fresh rosemary, optional

In a large stockpot over medium heat, heat oil. Add lamb pieces and brown, stirring often. Season with salt and pepper. Add onion, carrots and parsnips and sauté for 2 to 3 minutes. Add water and mix. Cover and bring mixture to a boil then reduce heat and simmer for 1 hour or until meat is tender. Add potoates and simmer for 15 to 20 minutes then add leeks and, if desired, rosemary. Continue to simmer, uncovered, until potatoes are tender, but not too soft.

Apollo 13

Movie Type: Adventure/Drama/History
Year: 1995

Rating: PG   Length: 140 minutes

Cast includes:

Tom Hanks, Bill Paxton, Kevin Bacon, Gary Sinise, Ed Harris and more

And the Oscar goes to...

☆ **Film Editing, Mike Hill and Dan Hanley**
☆ **Sound, Rick Dior, Steve Pederson, among others**

Brief movie overview

A dramatic tale based on the true story of the ill-fated 13th Apollo mission to the moon, and the men that rescued it with skill and dedication.

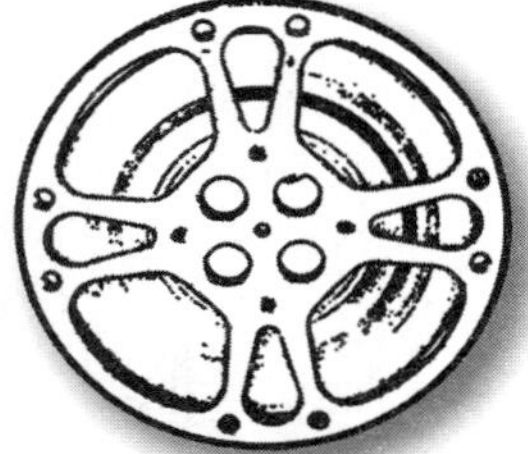

Flying Saucers

½ tsp. pepper
1 (10 oz.) pork tenderloin
¼ C. barbecue sauce

½ tsp. mustard
1 (7½ oz.) pkg. refrigerated buttermilk biscuits

Preheat oven to 425°. Rub pepper on outside of tenderloin. In a shallow roasting pan, place seasoned tenderloin. Roast for 15 to 20 minutes or until meat reaches an internal temperature of 160°. Remove from oven, and let stand 5 minutes. Shred pork. Reduce oven temperature to 400°. In a medium bowl, mix pork, barbecue sauce and mustard. On a lightly floured surface, roll each biscuit in to a 4″ circle. Divide pork mixture among 5 biscuits. Moisten edges of those 5 biscuits then top with remaining biscuits. Crimp edges with a fork to seal. Place saucers on a lightly greased baking sheet. Bake for 11 to 14 minutes or until golden.

The Nutty Professor

Movie Type: Comedy/Romace/Sci-Fi
Year: 1996

Rating: PG-13   Length: 95 minutes

Cast includes:

Eddy Murphy, Jada Pinkett Smith, James Coburn, Larry Miller and more

And the Oscar goes to...

★ Best Make-Up, Rick Baker and David Anderson

Brief movie overview

The grossly overweight Professor Sherman Klump is desperate to lose weight to impress a new colleague. He tests his special chemical formula on himself, which turns him into the slim, but obnoxious, Buddy Love.

Nutty Bourbon Chicken

½ C. finely chopped pecans

½ C. dry bread crumbs

¼ C. butter, melted

8 skinless, boneless
chicken breast halves

¼ C. Dijon mustard

¼ C. dark brown sugar

2⅔ T. bourbon whiskey

2 T. soy sauce

1 tsp. Worcestershire sauce

¾ C. butter, chilled and
cut into small cubes

½ C. sliced green onions

On a plate, combine pecans, bread crumbs and 2 tablespoons butter. Press chicken breast halves into the mixture to coat both sides. In a large skillet over medium heat, heat the remaining 2 tablespoons of butter. Place the coated breasts in the pan. Fry on both sides for 10 minutes each, or until chicken is browned and cooked through. In a small saucepan, whisk together mustard, brown sugar, bourbon, soy sauce and Worcestershire sauce until well mixed and smooth. Bring mixture to a simmer then remove from heat. Whisk in butter, one cube at a time. Serve chicken breasts and top with sauce.

Good Will Hunting

Movie Type: Drama
Year: 1997

Rating: R   **Length:** 126 minutes

Cast includes:

Matt Damon, Robin Williams, Ben Affleck, Minnie Driver and more

And the Oscar goes to...

☆ Best Supporting Actor, Robin Williams
☆ Best Screenplay, Ben Affleck and Matt Damon

Brief movie overview

Will Hunting, a genius mathematician living a rough life in Boston's south side, is discovered by a Fields Medal winning professor while Hunting is working as a janitor at a prestigious college in Boston. The professor enlists a psychologist to help Hunting discover his gift and the rest of his life.

Spicy Apples & Pork Chops

Will: Do you like apples?

Clark: Yes.

Will: Well, I got her number. How do you like them apples?

1 T. butter

1 onion, sliced

1 pinch red pepper flakes

1 apple, cored and sliced

2 tsp. sugar

2 T. balsamic vinegar

4 pork chops

Salt and pepper to taste

4 slices extra sharp Cheddar cheese

Prepare grill for high heat. In a medium skillet over medium heat, melt butter. Add onion and cook until soft. Season with red pepper flakes. Add apple and stir in sugar and vinegar. Simmer for 5 minutes or until apples are soft and golden. Season pork chops with salt and pepper. Grill for 3 to 5 minutes on each side until pork is cooked through. Spoon apple mixture on top of the chops then top with a slice of cheese. Cover grill and grill for an additional 3 minutes or until cheese is melted and bubbling.

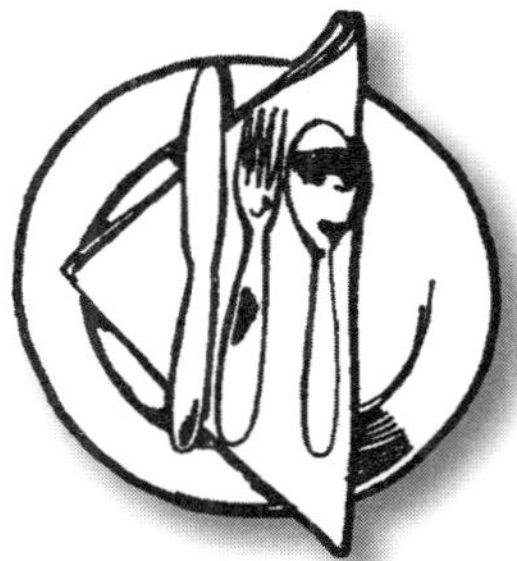

Titanic

Movie Type: Action/Drama/Romance/History
Year: 1997

Rating: PG-13   Length: 194 minutes

Cast includes:

Leonardo DiCaprio, Kate Winslet, Billy Zane, Kathy Bates and more

And the Oscar goes to...

☆ **Best Picture**
☆ **Best Director, James Cameron**
☆ **Art Direction, Peter Lamont and Michael Ford**
☆ **Also won for Cinematography, Costume Design, Film Editing, Best Score, Best Song, among others**

Brief movie overview

A fictional romantic tale of a rich girl and poor boy that meet and fall in love during the ill-fated voyage of the 'unsinkable' ship.

Filet Mignon with Mushroom-Wine Sauce

Filet Mignon was served to the 1st class on board the Titanic as a 4th course on April 14th, 1912. That same night, at 11:40 pm, the Titanic struck an iceberg about 400 miles off Newfoundland, Canada.

1 T. margarine, divided
⅓ C. finely chopped shallots
½ lb. fresh shiitake
   mushrooms,
   stems removed
1½ C. dry red wine, divided
1 (10½ oz.) can beef
   consomme, undiluted
   and divided

Pepper to taste
4 (4 oz.) filet mignon steaks,
   about 1˝ thick
1 T. soy sauce
2 tsp. cornstarch
1 T. fresh chopped thyme

In a nonstick skillet coated with cooking spray, over medium heat, melt 1½ teaspoons margarine. Add shallots and mushrooms, and sauté for 4 minutes, stirring occasionally. Add 1 cup wine and ¾ cup consommé. Cook for 5 minutes, stirring often. Remove and place mushrooms in a bowl and set aside. Increase heat to high and cook wine mixture for 5 minutes or until reduced to ½ cup. Add to mushroom mixture and set aside. Wipe skillet with a paper towel. Sprinkle pepper to taste over steaks. Once again coat skillet with cooking spray and melt remaining margarine. Add steaks and cook for 3 minutes on each side. Reduce heat to medium-low and cook for an additional 1½ minutes or to desired degree of doneness. Place on a serving platter and keep warm. In a small bowl, combine soy sauce and cornstarch and mix well. Add remaining ½ cup wine and consommé to skillet. Loosen browned bits on skillet. Bring to a boil for 1 minute. Add mushroom mixture, cornstarch mixture and chopped thyme. Again bring to a boil, stirring constantly for 1 minute. Serve with steaks.

The Cider House Rules

Movie Type: Drama/Romance
Year: 1999

Rating: PG-13   Length: 126 minutes

Cast includes:

Tobey Maguire, Charlize Theron, Delroy Lindo, Paul Rudd, Michael Caine and more

And the Oscar goes to…

☆ **Best Supporting Actor, Michael Caine**
☆ **Best Screenplay, John Irving**

Brief movie overview

Homer is a never-adopted orphan in rural St. Cloud, Maine. He is also the favorite of Dr. Larch, the orphanage director, who imparts his full medical knowledge on Homer. But Homer yearns for a self-chosen life outside the orphanage.

Apple Stuffed Chicken Breast

½ C. chopped apple

2 T. shredded
Cheddar cheese

1 T. Italian-style dried
bread crumbs

2 skinless, boneless
chicken breasts

1 T. butter

¼ C. dry white wine

¼ C. plus 1 T. water,
divided

1½ tsp. cornstarch

In a small bowl, combine apples, cheese and bread crumbs. Set aside. Flatten chicken breasts to ¼″ thickness. Divide apple mixture between breasts. Roll up each breast and secure with toothpicks. In a small skillet over medium heat, melt butter. Brown stuffed chicken breasts. Add wine and ¼ cup water. Cover and simmer for 15 to 20 minutes, or until chicken is no longer pink and juices run clear. Set aside. Combine 1 tablespoon water and cornstarch. Add to juices in pan, cook and stir until thickened. Serve stuffed chicken breasts with gravy.

Gladiator

Movie Type: Action/Adventure/Drama
Year: 2000

Rating: R   Length: 155 minutes

Cast includes:

Russell Crowe, Joaquin Phoenix, Connie Nielsen, Oliver Reed, Richard Harris and more

And the Oscar goes to...

☆ Best Picture
☆ Best Actor, Russell Crowe
☆ Costume Design, Janty Yates
☆ Best Sound, Scott Millan, Bob Beemer and Ken Weston
☆ Visual Effects, John Nelson, Neil Corbould, among others

Brief movie overview

A Roman general is betrayed and his family is murdered by a jealous corrupt prince. He comes to Rome as a gladiator to seek revenge against one man.

Caesar Salad

6 cloves garlic, peeled
¾ C. mayonnaise
5 anchovy fillets, minced
6 T. grated Parmesan cheese, divided
1 tsp. Worcestershire sauce
1 tsp. Dijon mustard

1 T. lemon juice
Salt and pepper to taste
¼ C. olive oil
4 C. day-old bread, cubed
1 head romaine lettuce, torn into bite-size pieces

Mince 3 cloves of garlic. In a small bowl, combine minced garlic, mayonnaise, anchovies, 2 tablespoons Parmesan cheese, Worcestershire sauce, mustard and lemon juice. Season to taste with salt and pepper. Refrigerate. In a large skillet over medium heat, heat oil. Quarter remaining garlic cloves and add to oil. Cook and stir until brown. Remove garlic from pan. Add bread cubes to hot oil. Cook, turning frequently, until lightly browned. Remove bread cubes from pan and season with salt and pepper. In a large bowl, place lettuce. Toss with dressing, remaining Parmesan cheese and seasoned bread crumbs.

Moulin Rouge

Movie Type: Drama/Musical/Romance
Year: 2001

Rating: PG-13   Length: 127 minutes

Cast includes:

Nicole Kidman, Ewan McGregor, John Leguizamo, Jim Broadbent, Richard Roxburgh and more

And the Oscar goes to...

☆ **Art Direction, Catherine Martin and Brigitte Broch**
☆ **Costume Design, Catherine Martin and Angus Strathie**

Brief movie overview

A stylish musical in 1899 Paris, in which a Bohemian poet falls for a beautiful courtesan who is also coveted by the jealous duke. Their romance is played out in an infamous club – the Moulin Rouge, a meeting place where slumming aristocrats and the fashionably rich mingle with workers, artists, Bohemians, actresses and courtesans.

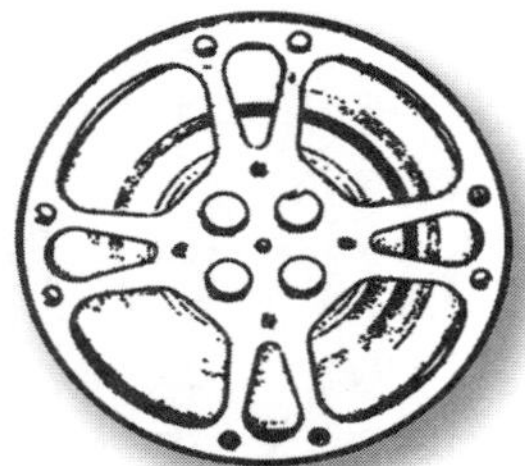

Slow French Dip

4 lbs. rump roast
1 (10½ oz.) can beef broth
1 (10½ oz.) can condensed French onion soup

1 (12 oz.) can beer
6 French rolls
2 T. butter

Trim excess fat from roast and place in a slow cooker. Add broth, soup and beer. Cook on low for 7 hours. Preheat oven to 350°. Split rolls and spread each with butter. Bake for 10 minutes or until heated through. Slice roast and place on rolls. Reserve juice for dipping.

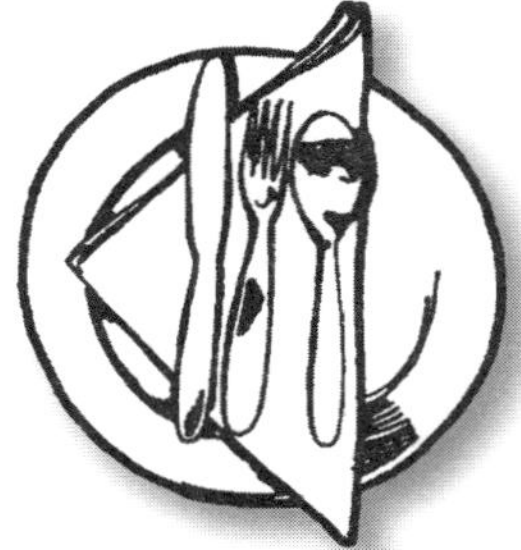

Chicago

Movie Type: Musical/Comedy/Drama
Year: 2002

Rating: PG-13 Length: 113 minutes

Cast includes:

Renée Zellweger, Catherine Zeta-Jones, Richard Gere, Queen Latifah, John Reilly and more

And the Oscar goes to...

☆ **Best Picture**
☆ **Best Supporting Actress, Catherine Zeta-Jones**
☆ **Art Direction, John Myhre and Gordon Sim**
☆ **Also won for Costume Design, Film Editing and Sound**

Brief movie overview

A musical tale of murderesses Velma Kelly, who killed her husband and sister after finding them in bed together, and Roxie Hart, who killed her boyfriend after realizing he wasn't going to make her a star. The ladies find themselves on death row together, as they fight for the fame that will keep them from the gallows in 1920s Chicago.

Chicago Style Pan Pizza

1 (1 lb.) loaf frozen bread dough, thawed
1 lb. bulk Italian sausage
2 C. shredded mozzarella cheese
8 oz. sliced fresh mushrooms
1 small onion, chopped
2 tsp. olive oil
1 (28 oz.) can diced tomatoes, drained
¾ tsp. dried oregano
½ tsp. salt
¼ tsp. fennel seed
¼ tsp. garlic powder
½ C. freshly grated Parmesan cheese

Preheat oven to 350°. Press dough along bottom and sides of a greased 9 x 13″ baking dish. In a large skillet over medium heat, crumble and brown sausage. Remove browned sausage with a slotted spoon and sprinkle over unbaked crust. Sprinkle mozzarella cheese evenly over sausage. Place mushrooms and onions in skillet. Cook, stirring frequently, until the onion is tender. Stir in tomatoes, oregano, salt, fennel seed and garlic powder. Spoon tomato mixture over mozzarella cheese. Sprinkle Parmesan cheese over all. Bake for 25 to 35 minutes, or until crust is golden brown.

Finding Neverland

Movie Type: Biography/Drama
Year: 2004

Rating: PG   Length: 106 minutes

Cast includes:

Johnny Depp, Kate Winslet, Kelly Macdonald, Freddie Highmore, Joe Prospero and more

And the Oscar goes to...

☆ Best Score, Jan Kaczmarek

Brief movie overview

The detailed experiences of J.M. Barrie, author of "Peter Pan", and his friendship with the family who led him to write the children's classic.

Picnic Fried Chicken

2 (2 lb.) whole chickens,
  cut up
2 C. milk
1 egg
2 C. flour

2 T. salt
2 tsp. pepper
3 C. shortening
2 tsp. salt

Rinse chicken with cold water, pat dry and set aside. In a small bowl, whisk together milk and egg. In a large resealable bag, combine flour, salt and pepper. Dip chicken in milk mixture then place in plastic bag, seal and shake until pieces are well coated. Remove chicken. In a Dutch oven, over medium heat, melt shortening. Fry chicken, in batches, for 10 minutes on each side or until golden brown and cooked through. Drain on paper towels. Sprinkle chicken evenly with salt before serving.

The Incredibles

Movie Type: Animation/Action/Comedy
Year: 2004

Rating: PG   Length: 115 minutes

Cast includes:

Craig T. Nelson, Holly Hunter, Samuel L. Jackson, Jason Lee and more

And the Oscar goes to...

☆ **Best Animated Feature Film**
☆ **Sound Editing, Michael Silvers and Randy Thom**

Brief movie overview

A family of retired undercover superheroes tries to live the quiet suburban life, but they are forced into action to save the world.

Mini Hero Sandwiches

2 T. butter, softened
4 hot dog buns, split
1 T. mustard
1 T. mayonnaise
4 slices deli turkey

4 slices deli ham
4 slices cheese
2 plum tomatoes,
   thinly sliced

Spread a thin layer of butter onto hot dog buns. In a small bowl, mix mustard and mayonnaise, and spread over butter. To assemble sandwiches, layer meats, cheese and tomatoes onto buns.

Walk the Line

Movie Type: Biography/Drama/Romance
Year: 2005

Rating: PG-13   Length: 136 minutes

Cast includes:

Joaquin Phoenix, Reese Witherspoon, Ginnifer Goodwin, Robert Patrick and more

And the Oscar goes to...

☆ Best Actress, Reese Witherspoon

Brief movie overview

A biographical overview of Johnny Cash's life, from his early days on an Arkansas cotton farm to his rise to fame as a country music legend, and all the dramatic twists of fate in between.

Walking Tacos

1 lb. ground beef
1 pkg. taco seasoning
4 (1 oz.) bags Doritos
1 small onion, chopped
Chopped lettuce

Shredded Cheddar cheese
Chopped tomato
Sour cream
Salsa

In a medium skillet, crumble and brown ground beef. Add taco seasoning and simmer until seasoning is absorbed and meat is cooked. Crush the Doritos in each bag. Cut tops off of each bag then add seasoned ground beef, onion, lettuce, cheese, tomato, sour cream and salsa, as desired.

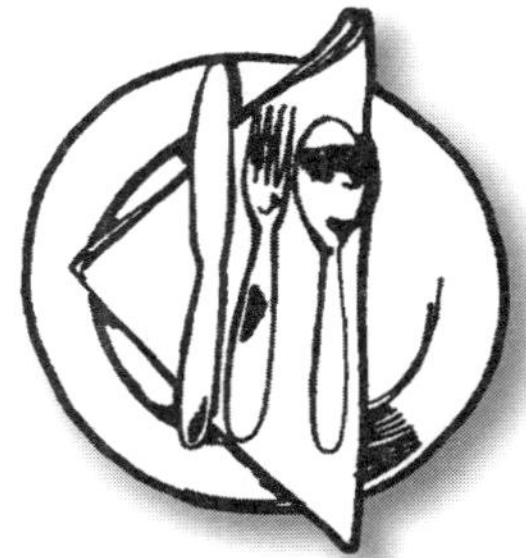

Memoirs of a Geisha

Movie Type: Drama/Romance
Year: 2005

Rating: PG-13   Length: 145 minutes

Cast includes:

Ziyi Zhang, Suzuka Ohgo, Ken Watanabe, Kôji Yakusho, Youki Kudoh and more

And the Oscar goes to…

☆ **Art Direction, John Myhre and Gretchen Rau**
☆ **Cinematography, Dion Beebe**
☆ **Costume Design, Colleen Atwood**

Brief movie overview

Nitta Sayuri reveals how she transcended her fishing-village roots and became one of Japan's most celebrated geishas. As World War II looms, Japan and the geisha's world are forever changed by the onslaught of history.

Smoked Salmon Sushi Rolls

2 C. Japanese sushi rice

6 T. rice wine vinegar

6 sheets nori (dry seaweed)

2 T. wasabi paste

1 cucumber, peeled and sliced

1 avocado, peeled, pitted and sliced

8 oz. smoked salmon, cut into long strips

Soak rice for 4 hours. Drain rice and cook in a rice cooker with 2 cups of water. Rice should be slightly dry. Immediately after rice is cooked, mix in vinegar. Spread rice onto a plate to cool completely. Place 1 sheet of seaweed on a bamboo mat and, using your fingers (may want to wet slightly), press a thin layer of rice on the seaweed. Leave at least a ½″ at the top and bottom edge of the seaweed uncovered. Dot some wasabi paste over rice. Arrange cucumber, avocado and smoked salmon over rice, approximately 1″ away from the bottom edge of the seaweed. Slightly wet the top edge of the seaweed and roll from bottom to the top, using the bamboo mat. Using a slightly damp and very sharp knife, cut roll into 8 equal pieces. Repeat.

King Kong

Movie Type: Action/Adventure/Drama
Year: 2005

Rating: PG-13   Length: 187 minutes

Cast includes:

Naomi Watts, Jack Black, Adrien Brody, Thomas Kretschmann and more

And the Oscar goes to...

☆ Sound Editing, Mike Hopkins and Ethan Van der Ryn
☆ Sound Mixing, Christopher Boyes, Michael Semanick, among others
☆ Visual Effects, Joe Letteri, Brain Van't Hul, among others

Brief movie overview

An obnoxiously ambitious movie producer in 1933 New York, tricks his cast and hired ship crew into traveling to the mysterious Skull Island, where they encounter Kong – a giant ape who falls for leading lady Ann Darrow.

Brazilian Braised Chicken & Bananas

2 lbs. boneless, skinless
   chicken breasts
2 T. fresh lemon juice
Salt and pepper
1½ tsp. oil
½ medium onion, chopped
3 plum tomatoes,
   seeded, chopped

Pinch of sugar
½ C. dry white wine
¼ C. chicken broth
1½ tsp. butter
3 firm-ripe bananas,
   halved lengthwise
¼ C. grated
   Parmesan cheese

Rinse chicken and pat dry. Rub chicken with lemon juice and season with salt and pepper. In a deep, heavy large skillet over medium heat, heat oil. Brown breasts on both sides until golden brown. Remove from skillet and keep warm. Add onion, tomatoes and sugar to pan and cook, stirring often, until tender. Return chicken to pan. Add wine and broth and bring to a simmer. Cover and simmer chicken for 45 minutes or until chicken is tender. Set aside and keep warm. In another large skillet, heat butter and sauté banana halves until golden brown. Arrange bananas over chicken and sprinkle cheese over all. Place over low heat and cover until cheese melts.

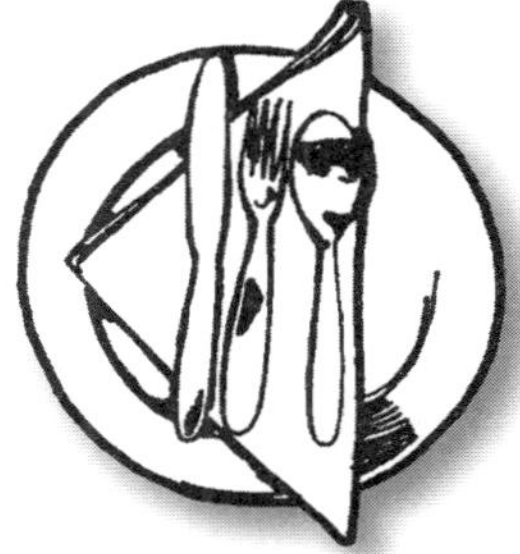

Movie Type:_____________________

Year:_____________________

Rating: _________   Length: _________

Cast includes:

____

____

And the Oscar goes to...

☆ ____

☆ ____

☆ ____

Brief movie overview

____

____

____

____

____

____

____

Ingredients:

Recipe Directions:

Movie Type:_______________________

Year:_______________________

Rating: _________   Length: _________

Cast includes:

And the Oscar goes to...

★

★

★

Brief movie overview

Fill these pages with your own Dinner & a Movie combination!

Ingredients:

_______________________   _______________________
_______________________   _______________________
_______________________   _______________________
_______________________   _______________________
_______________________   _______________________
_______________________   _______________________

Recipe Directions:

____
____
____
____
____
____
____
____
____
____

Movie Index

Recipe Index

Notes